PLAYING HURT
... Life Hurts but God Heals

LYNN WHEELER

Copyright 2023

All rights reserved. This book or any portion thereof may not be reproduced or used in any manner whatsoever without the express written permission of the publisher except for the use of brief quotations in a book review.

ISBN: 979-8-35090-145-0 (print)
ISBN: 979-8-35090-146-7 (eBook)

INFORMATION ON LYNN WHEELER MINISTRIES:

Lynn Wheeler Ministries
PO Box 1168
Mustang, OK. 73064

www.lynnwheelerministries.com

CONTENTS

FOREWORD BY PASTOR MAURY DAVIS 1

DEDICATION 3

ENDORSEMENTS 5

INTRODUCTION 7

CHAPTER 1   CHAOS OF 2020 9

CHAPTER 2   RESTORATION PROCESS 19

CHAPTER 3   SPIRITUAL IDENTITY CRISIS 24

CHAPTER 4   THE STORY 32

CHAPTER 5   POWER OF THE UNEXPECTED 41

CHAPTER 6   POWER OF WRONG BELIEFS 47

CHAPTER 7   WORSHIPING THROUGH MY PAIN 54

CHAPTER 8   GIFT OF PEACE 59

CHAPTER 9   UNFOCUSED VISION 67

CHAPTER 10   THORNS AND THISTLES 73

CHAPTER 11   BY HIS STRIPES 80

CHAPTER 12   PURSUIT OF REVIVAL 89

CHAPTER 13   BECAUSE OF MY DADDY 98

CHAPTER 14   NEAR THE CROSS 105

CHAPTER 15   MISSING CHILDREN 113

CHAPTER 16   THE TEST OF TRANSITION 121

CHAPTER 17	WAR OF WAITING	131
CHAPTER 18	MARRIAGE BUGS	139
CHAPTER 19	MY MONEY AND MY MAKER	148
CHAPTER 20	RELATIONAL REALIGNMENTS	156
REFERENCES		165

FOREWORD
by Pastor Maury Davis

I WAS FINISHING A TWO-DAY APEX LEADERSHIP CONFERENCE I WAS HOSTING IN Nashville, Tennessee without about 60 pastors and their spouses. The two days had been full of incredible moments, training, teaching, discussion and interactions. I gave the tables their final assignment…" Take the next 30 minutes and discuss your most painful moment in ministry…then determine what is the most painful experience at your table." Once the exercise was done, I realized there were people with tearful eyes and expressions of memories long buried. There were 10 tables and as I began to write the most painful experience the first table said…BETRAYAL. I then wrote eight out of ten tables who said betrayal was the most painful experience in their ministerial lives. The discussion ran deep and from heartfelt leaders the pain was unexpected, paralyzing at times and scarring always.

You are reading a book written by my friend and brother in Christ, Lynn Wheeler. This is a man I respect, honor and admire. I have known Lynn for decades and I have walked with him through injustice, unfairness and betrayal. I can tell you I have watched a man play hurt. Hurt in unimaginable ways and yet I watched him dust himself off, suck it up, put on the spirit of joy and continue to minister to other people. I know he felt the pain of rejection, unjust and unfair judgement. He had to feel like David felt:

Psalm 55: 12-14 "For it is not an enemy who reproaches me, then I could bear it; Nor is it one who hates me who has exalted himself against me, Then I could hide myself from him. But it is you, a man my equal, my companion and my familiar friend; we who had sweet fellowship together Walked in the house of God in the throng."

David is pointing out I did not see this coming. The pain is real! Betrayal and pain in walking with God should not be unexpected.

The danger in playing hurt is passing that hurt along. Great leaders in spite of their personal pain still possess the power and the passion to lift others out of their pain…the man, the brother, the man of God who wrote this book has not only experienced the pain he has overcome it. I do not know of anyone else I would rather learn from on this subject. As you read this book you will feel it, relive some of your own unexpected experiences and above all things realize you are not alone!

Pastor Maury Davis

DEDICATION

I want to dedicate this book to my daughter, Karissa. Karissa, I am inspired by you on a daily basis. From the moment you were born, you captured my heart, and I felt so much love for you immediately. That has never changed. It has been so wonderful to watch you grow in every area of your life. I am always here for you. I love you very much. You will always be "daddy's little girl."

ENDORSEMENTS

"In this life we experience pain. Whether the pain is caused by others or self-inflicted, we need God to heal us. My friend and mentor, Lynn Wheeler's new book, "Playing Hurt", will be a great resource for you and your loved ones to press on while you are praying for healing. God will return healing for your faithfulness."

Neil Kennedy
Author and Founder of Five Star Man

"I've been privileged to follow and lead hundreds and I've never met a single leader who hasn't, at some point in time, had to fight and play with one hand and attend to a personal wound with the other.

Playing hurt is a given for leaders and Christ followers desiring to do the will of God, accomplish something of value and leave a positive legacy.

Lynn Wheeler understands pain and how to turn it into fuel for the soul."

Terry Allen
Founder - MVP Leader Group

"Lynn Wheeler has been clearly communicating the Gospel for over 40 years. Lynn's creativity demands your attention, while his passion draws you to Christ. Many have been physically healed through Lynn's ministry and I believe many will be spiritually and emotionally healed through the book, "Playing Hurt…. Life Hurts but God Heals.""

Darryl Wootton
Oklahoma District Superintendent of the Assemblies of God

"I have personally been physically hurt many times while playing sports. I have experienced a turned ankle, broken and jammed fingers, and a torn ACL, which hurt the most. However, I never quit playing. I would heal up and keep going. Lynn's book, "Playing Hurt", will help you push through your mental, emotional and spiritual pain. It will help you to keep going even when you do not feel like it." (2 Cor. 4:8-9)

Pastor Kent Barnard
Grace Outreach, Rio Rancho, NM

"Lynn Wheeler sets the bar high on what it means to walk by faith, especially when you are "playing hurt." In this powerful book, we see how to be resilient in life and ministry as he models how to "rub some dirt on the wound, get up and keep going!" Lynn is a powerful preacher and dynamic communicator. His life and ministry are a living testimony that all things, even YOUR things, can be healed.

Pastor Greg Thurstonson
Dominion Church, League City, TX.

INTRODUCTION

I AM A HUGE SPORTS FAN. I ESPECIALLY FOLLOW FOOTBALL. I LOVE BOTH COLLEGE football and professional football. I spend time watching interviews, and I often catch up by watching ESPN. In the countless interviews of athletes, I have watched, there is often a common subject that arises. You see, injuries are part of the game. However, I have never heard one athlete complain about the "nagging" type of injuries that often come with playing a sport. I often hear them say things like, "I just push through the pain" or "We have to play hurt sometimes." It doesn't stop them. They just push through and play hurt. There is a difference in being injured and being hurt though. If you are injured it often leads to down time that requires time away from the game. I get that; however, I have watched many athletes play through the pain.

I realize that life is different from a sporting event. However, there are some analogies that apply to both. Life involves hurts and pain as well. We don't want to lie down and quit living because of the wounds we bear. We want to push through and PLAY HURT. The only way to do that is with the help of the Lord. Nobody is exempt from pain, but don't quit. Somebody else needs to hear your story. Keep pushing ahead. PLAY HURT! God will help us all.

Chapter 1

CHAOS OF 2020

THE YEAR 2020 BEGAN VERY NORMALLY FOR OUR WORLD. A FEW PEOPLE WERE GETTING sick, but after all, it was winter time. 'Tis the season for colds, flu, sinus infections, etc. However, this turned into a horrible pandemic very quickly when COVID began to manifest around the world. That pandemic brought chaos to our world on so many levels.

My wife (Dianna) and I were taking a team on a mission trip to Costa Rica in March 2020. We were flying through Charlotte, NC, and then on to San Jose, Costa Rica. Since March is also our anniversary month, we decided to go early and spend a couple of nights in Charlotte before we headed down to Costa Rica. I had always wanted to go through the grounds of the Billy Graham Evangelistic Association to see where he lived and hear more about his ministry. I have always had so much respect for him and his ministry. This visit was truly a highlight of my life. I sat in the video room and watched videos of him preaching and then giving an altar call. I wept as I watched hundreds of people respond and give their hearts to the Lord. I will always be grateful for that decision to spend a few days in Charlotte on our way to Costa Rica.

Our ministry center in Costa Rica is called "The Refuge." We are a part of "The Hope Project" there. We are trying to bring HOPE and HEALING to the less fortunate areas of Costa Rica. The Refuge is a resource center that provides parenting classes, limited medical services, English classes, counseling, and food and basic needs for children (diapers, formula, clothes, strollers, and more). We host teams on "short-term" mission trips a few times throughout the year. The teams are always a great help and such a blessing to our ministry there. If you have never been on a mission trip, you should consider it. It really is a "life-changing" experience.

While we were hosting our team in March of 2020, we began to get reports from friends and family back in the United States. The reports included the spread of a virus named Covid. It was making a lot of people very sick, and as a result, our world, as we knew it, was starting to shut down. Obviously, our friends and family members were concerned that the airlines would quit flying and that the borders of the United States would be closed. We had a meeting with the team and decided to stay and finish the trip. We did make it back home, but then the borders were closed two days after we made it home. We were all thankful to have finished the trip and to have made it back to our families before everything closed.

Suddenly, the Covid outbreak intensified all over the world. There were daily reports of people being hospitalized or dying. Businesses closed, and the governments were encouraging everyone to stay inside. If you did go out, masks were required everywhere. Fear gripped our world as we had never experienced anything like this before. Questions were being asked, but nobody really knew the answers. How bad is this? How long will it last? Questions without answers.

Children were confused as to why they couldn't go to school, and adults had no answer as to when they could go back. Sickness, heartbreak, confusion, and chaos were the themes of every newscast, and it was getting old quickly.

Then it began to affect the church world as churches were ordered to close, and meeting for church services was forbidden. I'd never dreamed that in my lifetime I would see churches shut down because of a worldwide pandemic.

This was my world. This is how I made a living. I must admit, I fought fear on a daily basis for several months. My health and my livelihood were in jeopardy, and the fear of the unknown was starting to grip our world.

As a traveling minister (evangelist), I rely on churches having me in for special services. The offerings from those meetings, which include revivals, marriage conferences, men's events, and retreats, is how I generate income and make a living. In 2020, I had twenty-two cancellations. That translated to twenty-two weeks with no income. It was nobody's fault; the churches were closed. They could not host a guest if they were not even having services. I was personally dealing with chaos all around me AND chaos within me too.

On top of everything, Dianna and I were separated from all three of our kids too. We also realize that it wasn't just us; our friends and family were struggling too. We knew God had our back, but the struggle was real, and our faith was being tried. Many of you can remember that struggle as well. It was a struggle mentally, physically, emotionally, and even spiritually.

As the months passed by in 2020, we seemed to be getting more knowledge of this virus, and we were all learning to live with the new restrictions. It still wasn't comfortable, but it was manageable. My heart broke for people that were losing loved ones and the ones that could not even visit their family in the hospital. It was such a difficult time. We were getting information, but was it true? Who were we to believe? We seemed to be on a merry-go-round that was picking up speed and would not stop. The chaos of 2020 brought a whirlwind to our lives and emotions that we are still trying to recover from.

Then we start having shortages of all kinds. Toilet paper was a big one. You couldn't find it anywhere. Hand sanitizer was sold out everywhere. Food items became scarce. All of that brought in a new level of chaos. I noticed that shortages also caused turmoil and unrest to surface. It seemed everyone was on edge, and anger began to set in. People were angry that they couldn't get what they needed or go where they wanted to, so everyone began to participate in the "blame game." Criticism of politicians and law enforcement officers became common. It really felt like a "no win" situation for everybody.

The chaos of 2020 was brought on and magnified by a pandemic. It was something I pray we never have to live through again. It brought so much more to our lives than I can cover in one chapter of a book.

At the time of this writing, we are just a few days away from entering 2023. So much chaos continues, and it truly has brought us to a place where we are "The Divided States of America." We are divided politically, economically, and, in many ways, spiritually. It seems that life is becoming increasingly chaotic on every level. The pace of life seems to get faster, problems are heavier, and the pressure continues to build. The chaos has made things hard, if not impossible, to manage. So many people are "playing hurt."

Sleep disorders, anxiety, depression, and deeply troubled hearts have become commonplace to the point that we almost accept them as normal now. We know life was not designed to be this way, and we are not built to carry this heaviness, so we hope and pray for reprieve. Yet, for many, it seems just out of reach. Oh, we seem to have our moments of feeling calm; however, feeling calm is not the same as finding peace.

Before her death, advice columnist Esther Lederer (Ann Landers) received about ten thousand letters a month from people requesting advice. When asked what the most common question she got in the letters was, she answered that "people seem to be afraid or worried about something." They were afraid of losing their health or their jobs, and many were filled with concerns about their families. Many letters she received described relational ruptures or family friction. In short, people were looking for peace and could not seem to find it, a situation that still persists today.

Peace is a very prominent theme in the Bible. In fact, the word "peace" itself is found in over four hundred verses in the Old Testament and New Testament. That doesn't count synonyms and allusions to peace throughout Scripture. Although it may be prominent in Scripture, peace remains elusive in many of our lives.

The Bible says, "The Lord gives strength to his people; the Lord blesses his people with peace." (Psalm 29:11)

Peace is a gift—a gift that must be nurtured and obtained through a relational connection with Jesus Christ. Peace is a blessing from God.

You may be asking the question right now, "How do I find peace?" Well, it depends on what kind of peace you are looking for. Many people do not realize that the Bible talks about more than one kind of peace. It actually talks about three different kinds of peace. Let's take a look at all of them in an effort to help us find peace and end the chaos.

First of all, let's take a look at Peace WITH God . . .

Romans 5:1 says, "Therefore, since we have been justified through faith, we have peace WITH God through our Lord Jesus Christ."

Isaiah 53:6 says, "All we like sheep have gone astray. We have turned everyone to his own way."

You see, a lost or unsaved person is at war with God. A lost person does not know peace WITH God because sin and God are at war with each other. Light and darkness cannot occupy the same vessel. Peace WITH God occurs when a sinner turns to God and is reconciled with Him. You may never find true, lasting peace until you meet the Prince of Peace!

Secondly, there is the peace OF God . . .

Philippians 4:7 says, "And the peace OF God, which passes all understanding, will keep your hearts and minds through Christ Jesus."

I like to define the peace OF God as "an inward spirit of tranquility and serenity of heart and mind that abides even in the midst of trouble and trial."

Sometimes we must trust the heart of God even when we cannot trace the hand of God. When you truly realize that God loves you and cares for you, and when you know that He will turn all bad things into good for you, then you can sincerely thank God even in the chaos.

I love the illustration of a ship that was sailing from England to New York. The captain of the ship brought his family with him for this particular voyage. About half way through, the ship found itself in a terrible storm that awakened the captain's little eight-year-old daughter.

"What's the matter?" she asked her mother. Her mother told her that there was a terrible storm. Almost without thought, the little girl then asked, "is Daddy on deck?" Her mother replied, "yes, sweetheart, Daddy is on deck." Immediately the little girl laid her head back on her pillow and went back to sleep.

May we ALWAYS REMEMBER that OUR FATHER IS ON DECK!! In the middle of the chaotic storms that are both in us and around us, God is still in control of the winds and the waves. He doesn't have to call for an emergency meeting with the Trinity or gather the archangels around for advice; God's got this! He is in control of what is happening in the world as well as our individual lives.

When we replace worry and fret with prayer and thanksgiving, we truly will experience what Paul was talking about in Phil. 4:7, "And the peace of God, which passes all understanding, will keep your hearts and minds through Christ Jesus." The peace of God is not the absence of trials; it is, however, experiencing God's peace in the middle of the chaos.

The third kind of peace in the Bible is peace with others THROUGH God ... this kind of peace represents harmony with other people that is a result of following biblical relationship principles. It's God's plan that His people be peaceable and live without strife and contention.

Psalm 133:1 says, "How good and pleasant it is when God's people live together in unity."

This requires us allowing God to produce HIS character in our lives. It is a process, and I think we all remain a work in progress on this subject. I want to do better. Do you?

So, we have talked about these:

Peace WITH God
Peace OF God
Peace with others THROUGH God

Let's bring some application now, starting in reverse order: peace with others THROUGH God ...

The world is trying to divide and promote chaos. People are wanting to argue at the drop of a hat. Road rage is getting worse. We can't seem to live well with people who have differing opinions than us. The two "hot buttons" seem to be politics and the vaccine, which is a result of the pandemic.

My wife and I took a vacation a few years ago to Durango, CO. During that vacation, we rode the train to Silverton, which you should definitely do if you ever go to that area of the country. Beautiful scenery.

Before we left the train station, a woman came on board to mention a few rules for us during the journey. It was all very basic stuff until she got to the very end. The last thing she said was, "There will be no discussion of politics on this train ride." A few of us laughed, and she quickly let us know it wasn't funny. She went on to say that the month prior to us being there, two men had begun to discuss politics, and it had turned into a fist fight. We all just sat there in amazement. Has it come to this? I sure hope not.

> **Nobody has ever walked away from a debate or an argument having changed someone's mind.**

Romans 12:18 says, "If it is possible, as far as it depends on you, live at peace with everyone." I think Paul is encouraging us to do our part to live at peace with others THROUGH God.

Let's make the application now to begin experiencing the peace OF God...

I believe the first step is to stop worrying. I have referenced this in other places in the book, but I believe it bears repetition.

> **Worrying is like a rocking chair; it gives you something to do but it doesn't get you anywhere.**

Worrying about a problem doesn't solve it, but it does keep the chaos alive. Chaos is the opposite of peace.

I believe the second step is to turn it over to God.

Phil. 4:6 says, "Do not be anxious about anything, but in every situation, by prayer and petition, with thanksgiving, present your requests to God."

I remember a song I heard many times as I was growing up in church. It was written as a poem in 1855 by Joseph Scriven, and the composer Charles Converse subsequently added the music in 1865 to its song version: "What a Friend We Have in Jesus"...

"What a friend we have in Jesus; All our sins and griefs to bear. What a privilege to carry everything to God in prayer. O what peace we often forfeit;

O what needless pain we bear, all because we do not carry, everything to God in prayer"

Paul's next step to finding the peace of God is to change your thought patterns.

Even though we may experience the peace of God described in Verse 7, we must constantly fight to not fall back into a pattern of worrying. That's why Paul goes on to say in Phil. 4:8, "Finally, brothers and sisters, whatever is true, whatever is noble, whatever is right, whatever is pure, whatever is lovely, whatever is admirable—if anything is excellent or praiseworthy—think about such things."

THE WORD IS THE BEST ANTEDOTE FOR WORRY

Isaiah said, "You will keep in perfect peace those whose minds are steadfast, because they trust in you." (Isaiah 26:3)

"For to be carnally minded is death but to be spiritually minded is life and peace." (Romans 8:6)

"Whatever you have learned or received or heard from me or seen in me—put it into practice. And the God of peace will be with you." (Phil. 4:9)

Paul's final step to experience the peace of God was to be obedient in what you had been taught. Obedience to God leads to peace.

Lastly, let's consider how to have peace WITH God . . .

Peace with God is obtained through Jesus Christ alone. Being a good person or doing good works is not enough. Praise the Lord for paying our debt by dying on the cross for our sins. You can have peace WITH God when you are in the right relationship with Him.

Do you have peace WITH God today?

Are you living with the peace OF God?

Do you have peace with others THROUGH God?

May the PEACE OF GOD cancel all the chaos in you and around you!!

Discussion questions:

1) Do you remember the effect the year 2020 had on you?
2) What are some ways in which it is still affecting you?
3) Do you sense an overwhelming amount of chaos AROUND you?
4) Do you sense an overwhelming amount of chaos IN you?
5) How can we keep what is going on AROUND us from getting IN us?

Chapter 2

RESTORATION PROCESS

WE LIVE IN A SOCIETY THAT WANTS EVERYTHING NOW. TECHNOLOGY HAS HELPED speed up the process, with some positive and some negative repercussions. At least once a day I hear someone complaining about the Wi-Fi being slow. If our "fast food" order is delayed at all . . . well, that is the end of the world. We can get food by driving through or even bank without getting out of the car. In a way, it is very sad the way our lives have gotten so busy that we need everything done quickly so we can move on to the next thing on our to-do list.

Wikipedia credits the invention of the microwave to a man named Percy Spencer. The microwave was invented after World War II from radar technology developed during the war. It was first sold in 1946 and, at the time, was called a "Radarange." The pictures of the first microwaves that were sold look nothing like what we have now. The initial microwaves were extremely large as compared to the contemporary ones.

We rarely see homes without microwaves today. We have found multiple uses for them, like cooking or reheating food, heating our coffee, and defrosting food. The bottom line is, we can do all of this much faster today because of the microwave.

Restoration does not happen that way. We think it should. We want it to. We even pray it will, but it does not. Restoration is a process. A long, never-ending process.

I know that some are thinking, "But Lynn, God has the power to change lives instantly." I agree. I have seen that happening many times in my ministry. However, you should know that God's work differs from our work. According to Romans 10:9, you can be saved instantly.

"That if you confess with your mouth 'Jesus is Lord,' and believe in your heart that God raised Him from the dead, you will be saved."

If you believe in your heart and confess with your mouth, you are saved. That is what we call in the church world "The Sinners Prayer." That is all you have to do to be forgiven of your sins. The price that was paid in full by Jesus on the cross has done that work. We cannot save ourselves; only Jesus has that ability. He paid the price, and He is not willing that any should perish but desires that all come to repentance.

God can save instantly. Heal instantly. Deliver instantly. Restoring and rebuilding are a process. There is a great example of this in the book of Nehemiah. The walls of the city had been torn down, and Nehemiah wished to rebuild and restore. When he got word that the wall of Jerusalem was torn down and the gates of the city burned (Neh. 1:3), he sat down and wept. (Neh. 1:4) Broken walls and gates had created a broken man.

We have all experienced brokenness in one way or another. Our spirits, minds, and hearts have been scattered and shattered into many pieces. Some of you reading this need restoring as you are broken and hurting even now. Others who may be reading are not broken but have been. You KNOW the restoring power of God! I know it! I am a living testimony that the brokenness that brought me chaos is now experiencing the peace of God. Please know that HE will restore you and give you back everything the enemy has taken from you. It takes time. Trust the process.

God put it in Nehemiah's heart to rebuild the walls and bring restoration to the city, which was experiencing extreme pain, confusion, and chaos. So, he started the process by meeting with the king to get permission to rebuild. In Neh. 2:5 he asked for help, and in 2:8 the King granted his request. I want you to know that in your restoration journey, THE KING is backing you up!! I am not talking about an earthly king; I am talking about the KING OF KINGS!!

Once permission was granted, Nehemiah went to Jerusalem and stayed three days (2:11). The process begins. Here are some things I want you to know about the process. It is my prayer you will have peace in the process . . .

1) Keep moving in the dark times . . .

2:13 tells us there were times Nehemiah traveled by night. However, he kept moving. Friend, keep moving even when you cannot see clearly.

Paul and Silas turned the jail into a jubilee AT MIDNIGHT! Keep moving.

The children of Israel were instructed to follow God. To help with that, the Lord put a pillar of cloud by day and a pillar of fire by night so they could keep moving even in the dark times. Keep moving.

The first gate he came to was the Valley Gate. Do not stop in the valley and pitch your tent. You are not staying there. Keep moving. The God that is with you on the mountain is also with you in the valley!

2) The devil will never stop fighting you . . .

He then went toward the "Jackal Gate." Jackal means dragon or devil. 1 Peter 5:8 says, "The devil is prowling around like a lion looking for someone to devour." He will never stop. Keep fighting. Greater is HE who is in you!!

3) Be faithful in "stinky" places . . . :-)

The next stop was the Dung Gate. Do you see the process? From the valley to the devil to the stinky places. Are we having fun yet? Not fun. It does seem as though there are a lot of "poo poo" problems that arise in the process. SOMETIMES YOU HAVE TO WALK THROUGH SOME THINGS YOU WOULD RATHER WALK AROUND. We would rather avoid the "stink," but keep moving. Never handle a "poo poo" problem with a "poo poo" attitude. Keep moving.

4) Hit the "refresh" button when needed . . .

In Neh. 2:14 they come to the Fountain Gate and the King's Pool. These gates bring the refreshing. You have been through a dark valley. You have fought the devil all day, every day. Hold your head up now, the fountain is in your future. It's the fountain that washes all the "stink" off and brings you a refreshing like only God can give. Receive that in Jesus's name!

5) Some things cannot come in . . .

Neh. 2:14b says, "There was no room for his mount." Some things we don't have room for. We are on a restoration journey and there is not room for the following:

Sin, hypocrisy, apathy, slothfulness, bad attitudes, and anger. Also, please realize there may not be room for some people in your life anymore. They are pulling you down and holding you back in your restoration.

WHAT I RODE IN ON NO LONGER WORKS, WHAT GOT ME HERE WON'T GET ME THROUGH!! Discern who and what continues with you on your journey.

6) Opposition will come from unlikely places . . .

In Neh. 4:1–2, Sanballat and Tobiah began to mock, ridicule, and criticize Nehemiah for rebuilding the walls. Nehemiah's response in Verse 6 was to keep moving and keep working.

Friends, some of your closest friends or family members may ridicule you on your journey . . . just keep working. Keep rebuilding your life. Handle the opposition with class and grace and keep moving.

7) Stay focused on the process . . .

Someone once said, "It is more effective to light a fire within someone than under someone." Nehemiah had lit a fire INSIDE his men. They kept working, strategizing, and planning. (Neh. 4:16–18)

8) Give God all the Glory . . . Neh. 6:15–16

Yes, there will be "stinky" places and times you have to back up and punt, but don't give up. Keep moving. God is rebuilding and restoring you! His PEACE will reign in your life. Give him glory for it!!!

A big part of you moving from chaos to peace is your restoration journey. Get ready!! God is about to give it all back AND MORE!! That is my FAITH declaration over you right now!! AMEN!!!

Discussion questions:

1) Have you ever witnessed the power of restoration?
2) Have you experienced restoration in your own life?
3) How can we get from our "pain" to restoration?"
4) What are some major oppositions on the road to restoration?
5) How is the "restored" you different from the "broken" you?

Chapter 3

SPIRITUAL IDENTITY CRISIS

IN 1995, DISNEY/PIXAR RELEASED THE FIRST ANIMATED FILM. IT WAS A MOVIE CALLED "The Toy Story." In this movie, a little boy named Andy had all of his toys come to life. The story line was built around the conversations the toys have. Among those toys was a dinosaur named Rex. Rex had an identity issue. After all, he was a dinosaur. People are supposed to be afraid of dinosaurs, right? The problem was that his inside didn't match his outside. Yes, on the outside he was a BIG, scary-looking dinosaur, but on the inside, he was soft hearted and lovable. He would even try to roar really loud to scare people, but it didn't work. Even when he gave it his best effort to be scary, the others would often respond with, "Oh, hey Rex." He wanted so bad for people to be afraid of him, but to no avail. Why? They knew who he really was on the inside. Once again, his inside did not match his outside.

I know a lot of God's people today who are living with a SPIRITUAL IDENTITY CRISIS. Their outside does not match the inside. On the exterior, they try to put on a smile and come off like they have it all together. However, on the inside, they are broken, hurting, and afraid. They have not dealt with many of the heart issues that plague them on a daily basis.

> A LIFE OF PEACE IS A LIFE OF REALIZING YOU ARE A CHILD OF THE HIGHEST GOD!

"For you did not receive a spirit that makes you a slave again to fear, but you received the spirit of Sonship. And by Him we cry, Abba, Father. The spirit himself testifies with our spirit that we are God's children. Now if we are children, then we are heirs—heirs of God and co-heirs with Christ, if indeed we share in His sufferings in order that we may also share in His glory." (Romans 8:15–17)

I think most of us struggled with our identity when we were younger. It was a time of trying to fit in and be accepted. When I was young, I would even go so far as to tell lies in order to be accepted.

I remember several instances of this. The struggle was real. I remember one time when I was a boy that our family went to another family's house for dinner. During the conversation, a story was told about a boy who had won a spelling bee contest in his school. When they heard that story, my parents went on and on about how awesome that was and how smart that boy was. So, guess what . . . In a few days I came home from school and announced I had won the spelling bee contest at school. I hadn't, but I still told them I had. I wanted my parents to go on and on about me like they had the other boy. I wasn't secure in who I was. That was not my parents' fault, it was mine.

In high school, it was all about getting the girl. I wanted to date this girl from another school, but another guy from her school also wanted to date her. I found out he was the quarterback of the football team. Guess what? Yep. I suddenly told her I was also a quarterback. I wasn't, but I told it. I wasn't secure in who I was. That was not this girl's fault, it was mine.

I grew up in church, and we had a youth choir that would travel and sing some in the summer. I didn't sing and still don't. You're welcome.

We went to this one church, and everyone in that youth group played an instrument. They were talking about it, and I felt like I had to say something to fit in. So, I blurted out that I played the bass guitar. I didn't, but I said I did. I faked it. Then one day it happened . . . I walked into church a little late one Wednesday night. My pastor, from the microphone, said, "Lynn, come on up here and play the bass." I had told everyone I played, but I didn't. It was embarrassing to say the least.

I had an IDENTITY MELTDOWN on more than one occasion growing up. I wasn't sure who I was. I wanted to fit in. I wanted everyone to like me. I was even willing to lie. Maybe you've had a similar experience? Maybe you are still struggling with identity issues? I continue to see these struggles in people everywhere I go. I am most concerned that more often than not, these identity issues carry over to our spiritual life.

> **WE DON'T KNOW WHO WE ARE BECAUSE
> WE DON'T KNOW WHOSE WE ARE!!**

I want to look at what I call the CIA of Identity . . .

COMPARISIONS: The reality is this: it greatly affects our identity if we constantly compare ourselves to others. Why? Because we always compare our worst to everyone else's best. We compare our lives to the lives people put on Facebook or Instagram. Really? That is only the aspect of their lives they want you to see. Remember that.

"If anyone thinks he is something when he is nothing, he deceives himself. Each one should test his own actions. Then he can take pride in himself, without comparing himself to somebody else." (Galatians 6:3–4)

Here is the main problem with the Comparison Trap . . . It affects our spiritual perception! We perceive that God must love others more because we feel they are more talented, etc. We think if we pray more, then God will love us more. The fact is GOD CANNOT LOVE YOU ANY MORE THAN HE DOES ALREADY. His love for you knows no bounds.

When I came out of Bible College, I was called to be an evangelist. I knew that, and while all my friends were accepting youth pastor positions, I was trying to book services. I started watching what I called "successful" evangelists. I thought if I copied what they did, then I would be successful. So, I preached loud and waved a hankie while I preached. It backfired on me because it was not who I was/am. I didn't really find peace in my heart until I started being me and preaching like me.

You and I will never be at peace with ourselves until we learn that being us is the best thing we can do. YOU are the best YOU there will ever be. Be YOU! Don't compare yourselves with others. God needs YOU to be YOU!

INFERIORITY: That means to "be less than." To be superior means to be "greater than."

As a traveling minister, I work with all different types of people and personalities on a regular basis. I have come across many people who believe they are "greater than" everyone else. Let's be clear; just because you outrank someone at work or have more money than someone, it does not make you "greater than" them as an individual. ALL people were created in the image of God, and before God, we are all equal. Again, we are talking about people here. I understand there are times we must submit to authority or follow instructions from those who are our superiors at work; however, on judgement day, we will all be on a level field with God, giving account for our actions. Besides, the Kingdom of God is about humility. Arrogance is the opposite of that. Someone once said that "Conceit is a disease that makes everyone sick except the person who has it." I agree.

Then I often come across people who feel "less than." They have been so degraded and beat down by others that they are mentally and emotionally crippled. They have been criticized all their lives and their self-image is destroyed. I pray these words get in your spirit, my friend . . . YOU ARE A CHILD OF THE MOST HIGH GOD! The opinion of others does not outrank the opinion of God. Not ever.

One of the greatest leaders in the Word of God had a real inferiority problem. He always felt he wasn't good enough. In fact, he had several conversations with God about it. You may know of him; his name is Moses.

In Exodus 3:10, God was sending him out, "So now, go. I am sending you to Pharoah to bring my people the Israelites out of Egypt." Moses' response was, "I AM A NOBODY." "But Moses said to God, "Who am I, that I should go to Pharoah and bring the Israelites out of Egypt?" In other words, God, I am a nobody. Get someone more well-known and popular. In Ex. 3:12 God assured him that He would be with him, but that didn't stop Moses.

Ex. 3:13 says, "Moses said to God, 'Suppose I go to the Israelites and say to them, 'the God of your fathers has sent me to you, and they ask me what is his name? What shall I say?'" God's response in verse 14 was, "I am who I am!" You see, not only did Moses feel like a "nobody," he also felt ignorant. Too ignorant to be used by God.

> **"EVERYONE IS IGNORANT, ONLY ON DIFFERENT SUBJECTS"** (Will Rogers)

In Exodus 4:1, "Moses answered, 'What if they do not believe me or listen to me and say, 'The Lord did not appear to you'?" Now Moses's argument is I MIGHT FAIL. Did you ever get in an argument with God? How did that work out for you?

Nothing seems to be working, but Moses keeps trying to explain to God why he cannot do what God has asked him to do. So now he is going to play the "lack of talent card." Ex. 4:10, "Moses said to the Lord, 'O Lord, I have never been eloquent, neither in the past nor since you have spoken to your servant. I am slow of speech and tongue.'" In other words, I AM NOT TALENTED.

Ok. Nothing is working here, so Moses will just come out and say what he has wanted to say all along . . . SEND SOMEONE ELSE! (Ex. 4:13) "But Moses said to the Lord, 'O Lord, please send someone else to do it.'"

So here is how an inferior person responds when God calls:

1) I am a nobody
2) I am ignorant
3) I might fail
4) I am not talented
5) Send someone else

Friend, God is looking for availability, not ability. If he calls you, He will equip you! You are His child.

Right now, I cancel off of you every critical word that has been spoken to you. Every harsh verbal attack on you is now deemed NULL AND VOID through the power of Jesus. You are NOT who or what they said you were.

We believe the Lord and His Word! Here is what the Bible says about you:

*** You are an heir of God.
*** You are the "righteousness of God in Christ."
*** You are "the head and not the tail."
*** You are "blessed coming in and blessed going out."
*** You are "above and not beneath."
*** You are "always lending and never borrowing."

What you heard said about YOURSELF in your childhood turns in to what you say about YOURSELF in adulthood. While growing up, people may have said YOU cannot do it. YOU are a failure. YOU will never succeed. Now you repeat it as an adult. I cannot do it. I am a failure. I will never succeed. AGAIN, I cancel those words that were spoken, and I decree and declare over you what the Word of God says about you!!

ACCEPTANCE:

When we were young, we did things to fit in and be accepted. Come to think of it, we do that as adults too. When we are not accepted, it affects how we view ourselves. Good news . . . God accepts us the way we are, but He does not leave us the way we are.

I spent many years believing God was sitting on His throne waiting for me to mess up so He could kick me out of His Kingdom. Then I read one verse that totally destroyed that concept. (Jer. 29:11) "For I know the plans I have for you," says the Lord, "plans to prosper you and not to harm you, plans to give you hope and a future." BOOM! Does that sound like God is just waiting to kick you out? He loves you. He values you. He accepts you. He has a plan for you!

In Matthew 3, when John the Baptist baptized Jesus, something powerful happened between God and Jesus. In Matt. 3:17 it says, "And a voice from heaven said, 'This is my son, whom I love: with him I am well pleased.'" God confirmed Jesus's identity. This is so important because in the very next chapter, that identity was challenged by the devil himself.

Matt. 4:3: "If you are the Son of God . . ."
Matt. 4:6: "If you are the Son of God . . ."

It was during a forty-day fast that the enemy came to Jesus and questioned His identity. However, remember Matt. 3:17? God had said He was the Son of God! God had confirmed it! Therefore, Jesus did not have to do any of those things the devil was asking as proof. He was THE SON OF GOD! His father had confirmed it already!

We, also, are children of God. It is confirmed by Romans 8.

Knowing it. Believing it. Living like it. That is a part of THE RESTORED LIFE!! Life does hurt . . . press on! Play Hurt because you are who GOD says you are!

Discussion questions:

1) What feeds our struggle with our identity?
2) Do you ever compare yourself to others?
3) Why do we often feel inferior?
4) Do you place a high priority on being accepted by others?
5) Why can't we believe what Jesus says about us?

Chapter 4

THE STORY

I HAVE ALWAYS BEEN A BIG FAN OF MOVIES. EVERYONE HAS THEIR WAY OF DESTRESSING, and this is one of my ways. I especially love movies that are true stories or based on actual events. Those types of movies have always appealed to me. I think I like movies because I like a good story. If I really like the movie/story, I will watch it over and over again. Children are that way for sure. If you have raised kids or you have grandkids, you know that if a child finds a movie they like, they want to watch it over and over again. When my daughter was small, I cannot tell you how many times in ONE DAY, 101 Dalmatians would turn into 303 Dalmatians!!

Then there is the other side of that word "story." Have you ever had someone say, "Oh, I told just a little story." No . . . you lied. That description of what they said is actually just a way to soften the reality of telling an untruth. Sometimes there is no harm intended, but it is still an untruth. For example, have you ever seen the road signs that say "Men Working" and they are NOT?! There may be one guy down in a hole, working, but everyone else is just watching.

Everyone in the world has a story. If we took time to listen to everyone's stories, they would all bring a different reaction. Some stories would make us laugh, some would make us cry, while others would make us think. Most of us have parts in our story where things get really ugly or complicated. Your story does not look like my story and vice versa. We have all had different struggles and life issues. However, even though our stories may be different, we do all have one thing in common. There is one thing that ties us all together. It is the fact that GOD WANTS TO USE OUR STORY FOR HIS GLORY!!

Let me ask you a few questions. Be honest:

1) **How many of you have told a lie? Come on, raise your hand; come on, right where you are, raise that hand. If your hand is not up, you are lying right now, so go ahead and raise that hand now.**
2) **How many have ever stolen something?**
3) **How many have ever been divorced?**
4) **How many have ever failed?**
5) **How many just want me to shut up, quit asking questions, and go back to writing?**

The reality is we have all failed. Your failures may not look like mine, and mine may not look like yours, but we have all failed. My story involves failure. A big part of "playing hurt" is letting God use your story for His Glory! We don't like to talk about our failures, but I have learned a couple of things since I started talking about mine publicly.

1) **It brings healing to me.**
2) **It brings healing to others.**

My story involves a marriage failure. My name is Lynn Wheeler, and I have been divorced. My first marriage ended in March of 1999. My third book is called "The Other Side of Courageous." I talk in detail about my divorce in that book. In short, here is how it went down for me. Papers were served to me . . . emotions overwhelmed me . . . some friends left me . . . God redeemed me!! There is power in God's redemption!! That is the only way you can live THE RESTORED LIFE! Life hurts, God heals. Keep playing even when you are hurt by past failures.

When I think about "restored lives" in the Bible, I cannot help but think about the Samaritan Woman. We don't even know her name. Preachers and teachers of God's Word only refer to her as "The Samaritan Woman." I like to refer to her because her story and mine are very similar. Jesus met both of us when broken relationships had complicated our lives. He met us at our point of need and met our needs. Jesus has and will meet us where we are and then take us where He wants us to be. RESTORED!

First of all, Jesus recognizes our need for friendship.

This story is found in John 4. For my first thought, I want us to take a look at Verse 6:

"Jacob's well was there, and Jesus, tired as He was from the journey, sat down by the well. It was about the sixth hour."

Let me point out a few things about this story that really add to this woman's story for me. You see, Samaritans are very ritualistic people. Not only spiritually but in everyday life. Every morning, the ladies would meet to go get water at the well. There were two reasons for this:

1) It was the cool of the morning, so it hadn't gotten really hot yet.
2) They were able to gather enough water to help them make it through the whole day.

You and I have just stepped into a story where a woman is coming to the well at "the sixth hour." That is straight-up noon. That is the heat of the day. Not only did she come when it was hot, she also came alone. Why would she choose to do both of these things? Come alone AND when it was hot? Perhaps she did it to be alone. You see, divorce was frowned upon then, and she had not only been divorced, but she had been divorced five times! Maybe she came alone in the heat of the day so she wouldn't have to see all the staring and glaring in her direction. Maybe the whispering and finger-pointing became more than she could bear. Her story caused people to push her away, and perhaps she just couldn't take it anymore. So, she came alone.

Let's go on . . .

"When a Samaritan woman came to draw water, Jesus said to her, "Will you give me a drink?" His disciples had gone into town to buy food. The Samaritan woman said to Him, "You are a Jew, and I am a Samaritan woman. How can you ask me for a drink?" (For Jews did not associate with Samaritans.)

Here is something else you may not have known. This takes this story to a whole new level here. You see, what the woman was pointing out here was also a cultural issue. Most of us know about the Jew/Samaritan mutual dislike for one another. What you may not know is that Jewish men were not supposed to speak to women in public. This is a powerful display of the character of Christ. He moved past the Jew/Samaritan issues. He moved past what the culture said about men speaking to women. He saw a broken, hurting woman with an ugly story, and He wanted her to know there was hope. Powerful!!!!

Let's go on . . .

"Jesus answered, 'Everyone who drinks this water will be thirsty again, but whoever drinks the water I give them will never thirst. Indeed, the water I give them will become in them a spring of water welling up to eternal life.'" The woman said to Him, 'Sir, give me this water so that I won't get thirsty and have to keep coming here to draw water.' He told her, 'Go, call your husband and come back.' 'I have no husband,' she replied. Jesus said to her, 'You are right when you say you have no husband. The fact is, you have had five husbands, and the man you now have is not your husband. What you have just said is quite true.' 'Sir,' the woman said, 'I can see that you are a prophet.'" (John 4:13–19)

You see, this woman's story included a long history of broken relationships. Five failed marriages. Think of all of the hurtful words she had had spoken to her in anger. Think of all the hurtful words that she, possibly, had said to herself. Think of the countless times she had felt rejection. Think of all the loneliness and feelings of being abandoned she must have experienced. Every relational disaster pulling her further and further down. She knew pain for sure.

Let me ask you these questions to provoke your thoughts to a deeper level regarding this story. Do you believe Jesus knew she had been married five times before He ever said it? Absolutely He did. Do you believe Jesus knew she was living with someone now who was not her husband before he ever said it out loud? Of course, He did. HOWEVER, He had now said it. It had now been spoken. This had changed the entire dynamic of this conversation. He knew it, BUT NOW she knew He knew!! Oh no!! What would His reaction be? She had an ugly, messy story . . . would He run away too?

This is what you will NOT see in this story. Jesus did not have this conversation with her and run! He knew it but did NOT say, "Lady, you have an ugly story, and you are one messed up chick! I am OUT OF HERE!"

No way! He knew her story but did not abandon her. If you are "playing hurt" in this area of your life, please know this . . . Jesus cares more about people that have been hurt or broken than religious rules or cultural issues. She needed a friend, and He was that friend. I needed a friend, and He was that friend to me too. You need a friend, and He will be that friend to you as well.

I was preaching in Mesa, AZ, a couple of months after my divorce was final. I was in the process of shutting down my ministry and taking a different career path. I was well into the interview process with another company, and I was making my own plans. I can visualize the smiles of the readers as I make that statement. It never works out when we make our OWN plans.

Anyway, it was a Tuesday afternoon, and I was sitting on the floor of the motel partly praying, partly meditating, and partly giving God instructions. (Here we go again . . . hahaha!) I was telling the Lord what we were going to do and when we were going to do it. YIKES!! In the middle of my "not so anointed" flow of instructions to the Lord, my phone rang. It was my friend John Davis on the other end. John was also my colleague in the ministry, and we had been friends for years. After exchanging greetings, John said, "Lynn, I was just praying for you, and I believe the Lord has given me a WORD for you, and I wanted to call and give it to you." Well, I must admit, my first thought was "I just told the Lord what we were doing!" He already knows. Again, I say "YIKES!!"

John proceeded to give me a WORD that forever changed my life and direction. He said, "Lynn, the Lord wants you know that as a result of what you have been through, there will be people walking out of your life. However, the Lord will send other friends into your life, AND they will be stronger than those that left." I begin to weep. I knew God was trying to get my attention to change my direction. I wasn't thinking clearly. The enemy had clouded my mind and told me the LIE that I could not continue in the ministry as a divorced preacher. I will forever be grateful to God and John Davis for being God's conduits to speak into my life.

As I reflect on those words today, the truth is, things have indeed played out just like that. My closest friends today were not even in my life at that time. As a follower of Jesus Christ, we all know that "He will never leave us or forsake us." However, we do need people in our lives that represent TRUE friendship. God knows that. He meets our need for a friend. Ask this Samaritan woman. Ask me. He truly is a friend that sticks closer than a brother.

Secondly, Jesus knows we all need to be forgiven.

This woman in John 4 is just like you and me. We don't just need a friend; we need a savior. We need forgiveness! She didn't need forgiveness because she had been married five times, but she needed forgiveness because we all need forgiveness. We didn't just need forgiveness the day we gave our heart to God, but we need forgiveness every day. "For all have sinned and fall short of the glory of God." (Romans 3:23)

I have to confess to you that I not only need forgiveness from God every day, I need forgiveness from other people too. I not only need forgiveness from other people, but I need to forgive others as well. I am asking the Lord for help in this area because it is such a big part of "playing hurt."

"Be kind to one another, tenderhearted, forgiving one another, just as God in Christ has forgiven you." (Ephesians 4:32)

Playing Hurt is not about casting blame or throwing stones at others. In fact, I believe too many Christ followers are playing the "blame game." It is always someone else's fault. "If they would not have treated me that way," "if they would not have left me," "if they would not have died," and so on and so on. Always blaming other people or circumstances for the place they are at in life. At some point, we must let it go! Why not today? Why not right now? Forgive others. It is a wonderful part of living life to its fullest even when you are "playing hurt." It helps you rest in the peace of God.

Thirdly, Jesus knows we all need a new beginning.

Let's return to our story in John 4,

"The woman said, 'I know that Messiah (called Christ) is coming. When He comes, He will explain everything to us.' Then Jesus declared, 'I, the one speaking to you, I am He.'" (John 4:25–26)

Now the conversation goes even deeper. The woman acknowledges that all of her life she has heard about the Messiah coming. She has been taught that when He comes, everything will change for the better, and so we are just waiting for Him. The next words out of Jesus's mouth were a revelation of who HE really was. He told this woman that He was indeed the Messiah (Christ).

In other words, He is no longer coming; He is here! The waiting is over, and now the Messiah is sitting here, talking to you. Here was the woman's response to this revelation:

"Then leaving her water jar, the woman went back to the town and said to the people, 'Come, see a man who told me everything I did. Could this be the Messiah?' They came out of the town and made their way toward Him." (John 4:28–30)

She was so excited to tell them about a man who had told her about everything she'd ever done but hadn't judged her. Neither had he condemned her or started treating her differently. She had had a very ugly story but Jesus had seen her a broken person in need of restoration. She'd came to the well for a drink of water but had found the living water! She had found a friend. She had found forgiveness. She now had a fresh start.

Maybe your dreams have been shattered and scattered in million directions, but today the Lord wants to give you a fresh start. Your story may be ugly and complicated, but it is not over!

"'But I will restore your health and heal your wounds,' declares the Lord . . ." (Jeremiah 30:17)

"He heals the brokenhearted and binds up their wounds." (Psalm 147:3)

> Always remember . . . LIFE IS A VIDEO, NOT A SNAPSHOT!

The enemy will always make it appear as if a single snapshot, that sin you committed or that one mistake you made, defines your life. A snapshot does not define you and your life. A snapshot would be the sum total of your story. Life is a video. That means it is still going on. You did not play (past tense) hurt; you are "playing hurt." The end has not yet been written. You can turn it around today. Jesus is ready to give you a fresh start. He did it for me. He will do it for you.

Your story continues, but today you can start by rewriting the end. An encounter with Jesus gives you a fresh start. It is hard to be at peace during our times of brokenness, BUT GOD RESTORES!!

"Because of the Lord's great love, we are not consumed, for His compassions never fail. They are new every morning; great is your faithfulness." (Lamentations 3:22–23)

> **GOD WANTS TO USE YOUR STORY FOR HIS GLORY!!**

Discussion questions:

1) Do you share your story with others?
2) Why do some people avoid talking about what God has redeemed them from?
3) What are the dangers of being hung up in the "snapshot" instead of understanding life is a video?
4) Do you feel as though that "your story" is a good lead-in to talk to others about the Lord?
5) Do you ever feel "judged" by other people because of your story?

Chapter 5

POWER OF THE UNEXPECTED

I HAVE BEEN SURPRISED MANY TIMES IN MY LIFE, IN SOME GOOD AND SOME BAD WAYS. I have had three surprise birthday parties in my life, where friends and families gathered to celebrate me on my birthday. Those are GREAT times and memories. I have also been blessed in many ways with surprise gifts or checks in the mail to help our ministry. They were unexpected surprises but very appreciated.

I have also experienced the POWER OF THE UNEXPECTED regarding bad news. I hear stories from friends and family of "bad reports" from the doctor. Of the death of loved ones or people losing their jobs. These "unexpected reports" cause our emotions to crash. At the time of this writing, two of these reports have literally rocked my world . . .

1) On Sept. 16, 2009, I was preaching a crusade in Enid, OK. It was a Wednesday, and I had literally just walked out of the pastor's office to head back to my motel to get ready for service that night. My phone rang and it was a board member at my father-in-law's church. He never called me, so immediately my heart sank. He then informed me that my in-laws had been in a car accident that my mother-in-law, Freda Linn, did not survive. My heart broke, and my mind went into a panic. I HAD TO GET TO MY WIFE! I was eleven hours away from her, and I knew she was devastated. At that time, we were living in Arkansas, and our home church

was Church Alive in Conway, AR. Our pastor's wife, Patty Long, went to our house to inform my wife Dianna. I was out of town and did not want Dianna to get the news by phone when she was by herself. We will always be grateful for Pastors Randy and Patty Long during that season of the "unexpected."

2) On Oct. 23, 2019, Dianna and I were spending the evening packing. We were leaving the next day for Colorado Springs, CO, where we were going to be speaking at a marriage conference. The mood in our home was light-hearted that night. We were excited about the ministry opportunity, and who doesn't love Colorado, right? However, in the middle of getting our clothes together for the trip, my phone rang. When I answered, it was my brother, Dennis, informing me that my dad had passed away. He had had heart disease. We'd been told by doctors that this was coming; however, we didn't know when. If you have been through anything like this, you know that even if you know it is coming, it is still "unexpected." The rest of the evening was a blur as we rushed across town to get to my dad's house. The unexpected had turned our joy and peace to heartbreak and chaos in one phone call.

"The unexpected" is powerful, and sometimes it can destroy your peace to a point that you are not sure you will ever feel comfort again.

I am so glad to know that even though Jesus is not here with us physically, He did leave His peace. John 14:27 says . . .

Peace, I leave with you; my peace I give you. I do not give to you as the world gives. Do not let your hearts be troubled, and do not be afraid.

You see, He had to go, but He left His peace!! I am so glad He did!!

Paul and his friends experienced the "unexpected" one day while at sea. The story is found in Acts 27, and I want to divide it into three events that brought about the "unexpected."

UNEXPECTED STORM

[13] When a gentle south wind began to blow, they saw their opportunity, so they weighed anchor and sailed along the shore of Crete. [14] Before very long, a wind of hurricane force, called the Northeaster, swept down from the island. [15] The ship was caught by the storm and could not head into the wind, so we gave way to it and were driven along. (Acts 27:13–15)

It was a nice day at sea. They had a gentle wind and weighed anchor. However, the UNEXPECTED happened. The hurricane force winds began to rage. Their ship was caught in the "unexpected" storm, and their lives went from calm to chaos in moments. In fact, the storm was so strong that they gave up fighting it. They just had to give way to it and let it take them where it would.

We all know what storms are. We have all experienced the storms of life. Some of you may be in the middle of one right now. For me, there have been times I have fought them so hard but finally couldn't fight anymore. I can relate to what happened to Paul and his men here.

> **STORMS DO NOT CHANGE GOD'S PLAN OR PURPOSE FOR YOUR LIFE!!**

The storms may be unexpected to us, but they are never unexpected to God. I know from personal experience that God is faithful in the peace AND the chaos. He is faithful in the calm AND the storm.

I want to confess something here. WOW, that got your attention!

I want to confess that after four years of Bible college and (at this point) forty years of full-time ministry, there are some things I still don't understand.

I want you to know that I don't understand the timing of God sometimes. I am not sure why He heals some people immediately, others gradually, and still others never.

I also don't understand why God sent an angel and got Peter out of prison but He left John the Baptist in and he got his head cut off. Did God love Peter more than John the Baptist? NO! That's absurd. Then why? I don't know. There are some things we will never understand.

Can I encourage you with this thought? Please don't seek to understand God, seek to TRUST Him! Proverbs 3:5-6 says,

"Trust in the Lord with all your heart
 and lean not on your own understanding;
⁶ in all your ways submit to him,
 and he will make your paths straight."

UNEXPECTED SHIPWRECK

Acts 27:41 says, "But the ship struck a sandbar and ran aground. The bow stuck fast and would not move, and the stern was broken to pieces by the pounding of the surf."

There are a couple of other things that I should mention now. First of all, Acts 27:27 tells us the storm lasted fourteen days. Also, Acts 27:33 says that the storm was so bad that they had not eaten for fourteen days. Friends, that is a LONG storm with no nourishment.

Not every storm I have been through has turned into shipwreck. There have been times I have been able to navigate the storm with the help of the Lord. However, there have also been times that my storm did turn into a shipwreck. I hit the "sandbar" and my life was broken to pieces. The unexpected storm turned into an unexpected shipwreck. Peace exited. Turmoil entered. I ended up "playing hurt."

I am sure that Paul and his men thought that they might be able to navigate the storm, but the situation eventually turned into shipwreck. So, when the ship was broken into pieces, that was it. Their mode of transportation was gone. The place of work was now gone. Now they were in a fight for their lives.

GREAT NEWS!!! God has a reputation of taking broken pieces (lives) and restoring them. He can take broken lives and bring them back together. He is not only the healer of our bodies, but He is also the healer of broken lives!

If you are reading this right now, and the storm you were in has ended in shipwreck, be encouraged; God is not finished with you. You are not finished, and it is NOT over! Please read on . . .

UNEXPECTED FAVOR

Several years ago, I wrote a book called "The F.O.G. is Rolling In." F.O.G. stands for Favor of God. That is still my most requested book and sermon.

Acts 28:1–2 . . . "Once safely on shore, we found out that the island was called Malta. The islanders showed us unusual kindness (favor). They built a fire and welcomed us all because it was raining and cold."

The storm/shipwreck took them to a place they were not expecting to go. Where were they? Would they be accepted or rejected? The Scripture says they received unexpected favor! Praise the Lord!!!

Luck –random occurrence
Favor—blessings from God

We have all gone through seasons when labor was high and favor was low. We have also experienced the opposite of that: We have experienced times in our life when favor was high and labor was low. Those are prime examples of the fact that it is God and not us. I would rather walk in the favor and blessings of God than depend on a "random occurrence" to bring good things into my life. I am praying you experience "unexpected favor" in your life often.

"The days are coming," declares the Lord, "when the reaper will be overtaken by the plowman and the planter by the one treading grapes. New wine will drip from the mountains and flow from the hills." (Amos 9:13)

"In his book, "The Speed of Favor", Tim Hill gives this insight on seedtime and harvesttime, "Any farmer will tell you that to get a harvest there is a time of working, a time of watering, a time of weeding and a time of waiting. Amos is speaking to the farmers who know it takes four months for the harvest after the planting season, but he is prophesying the harvest and seed planting are coming together."[1]

My prayer for you is that you might live in peace in spite of the "unexpected storms." I pray that God will:

- a) Exceed all that you expect in Jesus's name
- b) Restore the shipwrecks of your life
- c) Multiply all that you invest/sow/give
- d) Accomplish His work in your life with acceleration
- e) Cause you to walk in His favor with victory over the enemy

> **GOD'S PEACE IS NOT THE CALM AFTER THE STORM, IT'S THE STEADFASTNESS DURING IT!!**

Discussion questions:

1) Have you experienced "unexpected" storms?
2) Have any of those storms led to shipwreck?
3) What were some survival instincts that kicked in?
4) In reflection, can you see how God used it for your good?
5) Do you ask God for favor in every area of your life?

---

[1] "The Speed of Favor" by Tim Hill Copyright ©2018 by Dr. Timothy M. Hill, used by permission of Charisma House Publishing

Chapter 6

POWER OF WRONG BELIEFS

THE CHILDREN OF ISRAEL HAD CROSSED THE RED SEA IN EXODUS 14. HOWEVER, EVEN after being a part of a supernatural miracle, they became discontent. In Exodus 16:2,3, the Scriptures tell us, "In the desert the whole community grumbled against Moses and Aaron. The Israelites said to them, 'If only we had died by the Lord's hand in Egypt! There we sat around pots of meat and ate all the food we wanted, but you have brought us into this desert to starve this entire assembly to death."

Now you and I both know this is NOT TRUE. Moses and Aaron DID NOT bring them into the desert to starve them. We KNOW that. However, they thought it WAS TRUE. It was a "wrong belief." Even though it was false, they still believed it.

Friends, wrong beliefs are powerful, and they play a huge part in robbing us of our peace. Wrong beliefs are powerful both individually and corporately. In other words, we are believing what isn't true, so that's killing our peace. It magnifies "playing hurt."

I recently saw a bumper sticker on a car that said, "If Jesus said it, I believe it, and that makes it so." I have to tell you that I disagree. The truth is that if Jesus said it, that makes it so; it doesn't matter whether I believe it or not. For God and His Word are the foundation for all truth.

Jesus said, "I am the way, the TRUTH and the life."

Wrong beliefs bring chaos, right beliefs bring peace!

Our belief system also affects the way we act and the way we talk. Our beliefs have to change before our behavior will change. Wrong beliefs will bring wrong behavior. In other words, it is what we believe on the inside that drives our actions. The grumbling and complaining that the children of Israel were doing was all based on a wrong belief. They taught us that it is possible to get out of Egypt (land of bondage) but not get Egypt out of you.

As I read through this story, I located three WRONG BELIEFS that I believe contributed to a lack of peace and forty years of wandering in the desert. Let me show what I found . . .

1) I CAN ONLY RELY ON ME

Exodus 16:4, "Then the Lord said to Moses, 'I will rain down bread from heaven for you. The people are to go out each day and gather enough for that day. In this way, I will test them and see whether they will follow my instructions.'"

The Lord was trying to show them that it was not all on them. It was THE LORD who provided by raining down manna on them.

The Lord is still our ultimate provider! God is our source; everything else is just a resource. "Some trust in chariots and some in horses, but we trust in the name of the Lord our God." (Psalm 20:7)

I attended Bible College in Springfield, MO, from 1978 to 1982. Right next door to our campus was a place called Maranatha Village. Maranatha Village was a retirement place for retired ministers/missionaries to come and live once they'd completed their active ministry. My final year of college, our professor gave us an assignment that I thought was going to be an easy A.

The assignment was that we would be given a piece of paper with the name of a minister who now lived at Maranatha Village. We were told his name, where he lived, and even given the questions to ask him. Sounded easy enough. I just had to go there, ask the questions, and record the answers.

The day of the interview came. I was going to be interviewing a former missionary. I have to confess that I was totally focused on getting in, asking the questions, and getting to Pizza Hut.

Don't judge, I was a college kid.

When I walked in, I was greeted by a very nice gentleman. He invited me sit on the couch and immediately informed me that his wife had passed away, which was why he was alone for the meeting. After a short period of "small talk," I began my interview.

I starting asking questions, and he was answering quickly. I was writing fast. When he stopped talking, I would ask the next question. I hardly looked up for the first five minutes or so. Then we got to the fifth question,

"Sir, what is the greatest miracle you've ever seen in your ministry?" Even as I asked the question, I was still looking down, writing down his answer from the previous question. For the first time since I had arrived, there was silence.

It took me a minute to realize it, and when I looked up, I saw tears streaming down the face of this retired missionary. I laid my materials aside and sat up on the edge of the couch. I said, "Sir, please take your time. I really do want to hear the answer to this question."

It took a few minutes for him to gain his composure. Once he could talk, he told me a story. Before I share it though, I would like to remind you that he'd been a missionary in the 40s, 50s, and 60s. There was no Facetime calling then. No Zoom. No PayPal or CashApp. No social media. Missionaries then had to leave their friends and families behind. They would get perhaps an occasional phone call back home when they could afford it. Keep this in mind as I tell his story . . .

He told me one day he was in his office at his house. His wife came in around dinner time and informed him that they had no food in the house and no money to buy any. She reminded him that he had two daughters in the other room that were hungry and they needed to eat.

He said he told his wife to go set the dinner table just as if they were going to eat. Put out plates, dishes, and silverware. She did and then called the family to the table. They sat down and the girls began to ask where the food was. He had his family join hands and pray for food that was not there. As soon as he said "AMEN," there was a knock at the door. His wife went to the door, and nobody was there. She knew she'd heard a knock, so she walked out into the yard and looked up and down the street. Nobody. When she turned and walked back on the porch, she saw two bags of groceries sitting there!! She brought them in, and as they unpacked the sacks, they discovered there was enough food to eat for two weeks!!

The missionary was crying, and I was crying. As a young preacher who never even knew what it was to go without food, this story made a lasting impression on me. GOD IS OUR PROVIDER!!

If you are a child of God, please know that you are not alone! The devil may want you to think that God has deserted you, but He hasn't. It is not all on you. God is working on your behalf. The children of Israel believed it all depended on them, and that was a WRONG BELIEF. Don't you believe it too.

2) I AM GOING TO COME UP SHORT

The Lord had given the instructions to get what you need but not more than you need. Exodus 16:19–20 says, "Then Moses said to them, 'No one is to keep any of it until morning.' However, some of them paid no attention to Moses; they kept part of it until morning, but it was full of maggots and began to smell. So, Moses was angry with them."

Even though God gave specific instructions, they disobeyed because they believed they were not going to have enough. When we believe we are going to come up short, it affects our actions. The result of the "wrong belief" was that the manna had maggots and began to smell. The Lord had promised them "daily bread," but they did not believe it. Wrong beliefs triggered disobedience am the end result was a bit "stinky."

Several years ago, I was single and living alone. I left on a twelve-day mission's trip to Russia. When I got home, I discovered I had left a dish in the refrigerator. It was in one of those containers you can't see through. It had made its way to the back and I'd forgotten what was in there. I opened it up to discover it was leftover tuna salad. YIKES!!! It was the most horrible smell you can imagine. It was so bad that I threw out the WHOLE container!! Nothing would ever live in that container again!!

When I read about the disobedience that caused the manna to be full of maggots and begin to smell, I also think about that twelve-day old tuna salad. Not a pleasant memory.

3) I CAN ALTER GOD'S INSTRUCTIONS TO FIT MY SITUATION

This is the third "wrong belief" that I find in this story. You may be thinking this contradicts my first wrong belief. Hear me out. God gave them the instructions but He couldn't carry it out for them. THEY had to do that.

So, God changed the instructions in Exodus 16:23: "He said to them, 'This is what the Lord commanded: tomorrow is to be a day of Sabbath rest, a holy Sabbath to the Lord. So, bake what you want to bake and boil what you want to boil. Save whatever is left and keep it until morning.'"

The following blows me away. Let's keep going, "So they saved it until morning and it did not stink or get maggots in it. 'Eat it today,' Moses said, 'because today is the Sabbath to the Lord. You will not find any of it on the ground today. Six days you are to gather it, and on the seventh day, the Sabbath, there will not be any. Nevertheless, some of the people went out on the seventh day to gather it, but they found none. Then the Lord said to Moses, 'How long will you refuse to keep my commands and my instructions? Bear in mind that the Lord has given you the Sabbath; that is why on the sixth day he gives you bread for two days. Everyone is to stay where they are on the seventh day; no one is to go out.' So, the people rested on the seventh day." (Exodus 16:24–30)

Verse 27 blows me away! They still were not following the instructions of God. Finally, Moses got them to obey.

It is the six-day principle. Six days we work, and we rest on the seventh. Obey God and manage our manna and everything will be alright. God won't do it all for us. We must do our part.

I recently saw a video of two people stuck on an escalator. When the escalator in the mall stopped, they just stood there and called for help. Over and over. Stood there for several minutes. The point is both profound and humorous. Step up and step off!! You can do it!

I pray you are released of wrong thinking that leads to wrong beliefs. If your belief system is low or nonexistent, just remember, you can never go wrong by following God's instructions. They work!

Discussion questions:

1) Have you ever believed something to be true and then found out it wasn't? How did you handle that?
2) Why do you think the Children of Israel had such a hard time believing God?
3) Do you believe that faith is an action?
4) Do you believe the statement "If we do our part, God will do His?"
5) Do you struggle with "murmuring and complaining" during those times of waiting for God?

Chapter 7

WORSHIPING THROUGH MY PAIN

IN MATTHEW 22:36–38, JESUS WAS ASKED, "TEACHER, WHICH IS THE GREATEST commandment in the law? Jesus replied, "Love the Lord your God with all your heart and with all your soul and with all your mind. This is the first and greatest commandment."

I have discovered that following Jesus's instructions here helps me live in peace in every area of my life. The chaos comes when I stray from them.

Jesus is basically asking us to LIVE A LIFE OF WORSHIP. Worship when we do not feel like it. Worship when our pain is unbearable. I must also mention that a LIFE OF WORSHIP is different that a MOMENT of worship. It is sitting at His feet, not just having a moment during worship at church or listening to a favorite worship song while driving down the road. Sit at His feet. Listen. Learn. Just be in HIS presence. Peace comes from HIS presence.

A great illustration of this is the story of the demon who possessed man. The Scripture says, "And the people went out to see what had happened. When they came to Jesus, they found the man from whom the demons had gone out, sitting at Jesus's feet, dressed and in his right mind; and they were afraid." (Luke 8:35)

So many people are faithful to church and God when they have a need. However, when the need is met, they are gone. That's both sad and heartbreaking. We do not worship Jesus because of what He does for us; we worship Him because of who He is! This man had many demons cast out of him, and we find him "sitting at the feet of Jesus." That's living a life of worship.

Let me ask you, whose feet are you sitting at? Who or what are listening to? Hollywood? Government? During the pandemic year of shutdown (2020), our eyes were glued to the news. These things are not wrong unless that's where you spend ALL your time. I do wonder though, did your Bible reading increase? Did your prayer time increase? I repeat . . . peace comes from HIS presence. When we are truly worshipping Him, it requires sitting at His feet more than anywhere else. If we do that, it turns us from MOMENTS of worship to a LIFESTYLE of worship.

What does a life of worship look like? I want to stay with this same story to shed light on that question . . .

FIRST of all, a person who worships through their pain experiences a life transformation. Most of us cannot relate to being "demon possessed," but we can relate to a "life transformation." The verse I shared above (Luke 8:35) tells us the man that had been demon possessed was now "sitting at the feet of Jesus, dressed and in his right mind." We are reading about a man whose life was truly CHANGED. A true encounter with Jesus will change your life.

Even though my schedule does not allow me to be there often, my home church is People's Church in Oklahoma City, OK. My pastor is Herbert Cooper, and he says at every single service that our church is all about "MORE CHANGED LIVES!" It is my prayer that this is the heart of every church.

It is OK to not be OK. If you have hurts, habits, or hang ups, Jesus is the answer. HE can truly change lives. He is truly the Prince of Peace!

If we go back to Luke 8:27, we find out how bad this man really was: "When Jesus stepped ashore, He was met by a demon-possessed man from the town. For a long time, this man had not worn clothes or lived in a house but had lived in the tombs." So, he goes from that condition to "sitting at Jesus's feet, dressed and in his right mind." How? His life was truly changed!! He is now sitting at the feet of Jesus because living a life of worship is a continual process.

MORE CHANGED LIVES!!!!

Secondly, we obey His instructions . . .

Now we see that Jesus is about to get on a boat to return home. Luke 8:38–39 says, "The man from whom the demons had gone out begged to go with Him, but Jesus sent him away saying, 'Return home and tell how much God has done for you.' So, the man went away and told all over town how much Jesus had done for him."

Living a life of obedience is a constant battle between the flesh and spirit. When the flesh is winning that battle, it creates more opportunities for turmoil and chaos, which creates more pain. Following the flesh eventually leads to pain. How can we ensure a victory for the spirit instead of the flesh? By feeding the Spirit man more than your flesh. Whatever we feed the most, grows the fastest. Feed the Spirit. Cancel chaos. That is the obedient life.

Thirdly, allow your pain to preach . . .

Let's look at the timeline again:

Luke 8:35 . . . we read that people saw this man sitting at the feet of Jesus.

Luke 8:36 . . . "Those who had seen it told the people how the demon-possessed man had been healed."

This man is now witnessing with his actions and life.

Dianna and I have dear pastor friends who recently lost their son in a tragic work accident. He was twenty-five years old and had been married for less than two years. Very sad and painful situation. We were blessed to be ministry guests in their church a few months after the accident. As they were telling us the details of the accident, one story stood out to me . . .

A friend of the young man who was killed said to the father (my pastor friend), "Your son preached to me every day without saying a word." That was so powerful to me. In the middle of experiencing pain beyond comprehension, our friends needed that powerful story of their son witnessing with his actions. We will never understand why his life ended so young, but his short life made a difference in others' lives when he didn't even open his mouth.

There is a popular saying in the church world that goes thus: "Do your best to preach every day and when necessary, use words."

The demon-possessed man was now winning souls by the way he lived his life. He was preaching even while he was "playing hurt."

That is what attracts others. Lost and broken people are attracted to changed lives. People whose lives have been changed by Jesus cannot help but tell others. The demon-possessed man obeyed Jesus and went to tell the whole town what the Lord had done for him. He witnessed with his life and with his words. He told his story in a way that touched others. So, when Jesus returned, they welcomed Him!

"Now when Jesus returned, a crowd welcomed Him. They were expecting Him." (Luke 8:40)

Preaching with and through our pain means that we do not keep Jesus a secret. Yes, you are "playing hurt," and so am I, but let's let Jesus shine through our lives and not our pain. Let the way you live your life "preach" loudly.

Discussion questions:

1) Does our pain keep us from worshipping God at times?
2) Do you struggle with pushing through pain to praise HIM?
3) What speaks to you most about the story of the man who was demon possessed?
4) Is it possible for others to "see" the work the Lord has done in us?
5) Is the "Spirit/Flesh" battle daily or occasional?

Chapter 8

GIFT OF PEACE

AT THE TIME OF THIS WRITING, I HAVE JUST HAD ANOTHER BIRTHDAY (JULY 4). The older I get; the more do I value gifts. However, with age, the types of gifts I value have certainly changed. When I was young, it was all about opening the presents or opening the card with money in it. While I still appreciate those things, my greatest gifts now include being with the people I love. If I can have all my family together, that would be my most cherished gift of all.

When Jesus left this earth, He left us a gift. A gift that we need now more than ever. He left us the GIFT OF PEACE! In John 14:27, Jesus told us that He had to leave but that He would leave us a comforter. That comforter is our peace in the midst of chaos. If Jesus left that peace for us, then He knew we would need it. "Playing hurt" has brought a lot of chaos into our lives; however, I am so grateful for the comforter that still brings peace in the middle of the storms.

The prophet Isaiah prophesied the birth of Jesus in Isaiah 9:6. One of the names that Isaiah said Jesus would be known as was the "Prince of Peace." He announced his birth and then called Him the "Prince of Peace." That is somewhat humorous to me because NO BIRTH is peaceful. I was in the room when my daughter was born; it was not peaceful. I am sure the birth of Jesus was not peaceful either.

PLAYING HURT... Life Hurts but God Heals

There are so many people who associate the birth of Jesus with "peace on earth and good will to men." However, that is actually not in Scripture. That phrase is only mentioned one time in the Bible (Luke 12:51), but it is not in relation to the birth of Christ. The Bible does not say that Jesus came to bring peace on earth, but it does say that He came to give you the gift of peace. (John 14:27) Jesus gave His life for people, not places.

Also, before I move on from this thought, I want to share something I have personally experienced in my spiritual journey. I have witnessed a shift in the atmosphere on a number of occasions. I have walked into a situation where there was strife, chaos, or turmoil, and I have prayed for an atmosphere shift. I would pray the same way Jesus did when He spoke to the storm: "Peace, Be Still." If the same power that raised Christ from the dead dwells in us, then we can speak to the storm in the same way! Jesus is still the PEACE SPEAKER in your life, my friend. He left you the gift of peace. It's yours. Receive it.

Here is how the birth of Jesus was announced in Luke 2:11–14: "Today in the town of David a Savior has been born to you; He is the Messiah, the Lord. This will be a sign to you: You will find a baby wrapped in clothes and lying in a manger." Suddenly a great company of the heavenly hosts appeared with the angel, praising God and saying, "Glory to God in the highest heaven, and on earth peace to those on whom His favor rests." May HIS PEACE be present in your life always. May HIS PEACE fill your home and your workplace. May HIS PEACE guide you all the days of your life!!

I have observed some things that seem to disrupt peace in our lives. These are things that sometimes make us feel like we have lost the "gift" that Jesus left us. In this chapter, I want to talk about the four "peace disruptors" I see the most ...

1) Uncontrollable Circumstances

"Disaster follows disaster; the whole land lies in ruins. In an instant my tents are destroyed, my shelter in a moment." (Jer. 4:20)

In that verse Jeremiah reminds us how quickly things can change. How in an INSTANT something can happen that takes away our peace. One report from a doctor. One phone call. We have all experienced uncontrollable circumstances. Some don't directly affect us but still affect our peace. For example:

a) People who walk into churches and start shooting
b) People who start shooting into a crowd of people simply attending a concert.
c) Hurricanes/floods/tornadoes
d) Cancer, car wrecks, loss of employment

The truth is, there are things we will never understand. Horrible circumstances that are out of our control. Whether they directly impact us or not, they sure affect our peace.

Several years ago, I was invited to speak at a pastors' conference in Haiti. My wife and I went a few days early and visited a ministry center. We enjoyed walking through the center and seeing all of the different ministries that they were doing. We came to one room and the person giving us the tour told us that that particular room had been set up as a medical room after the 2010 earthquake that killed some 270,000 people. They'd brought people there that were wounded in hopes of saving their lives.

Several doctors from the United States had got on a plane to Haiti to help. A surgeon from Texas had been working in that particular room. They'd brought in a couple of ladies that had had a building collapse on their legs. The doctor had come in, looked at them both, and then stepped in the hallway to talk to the nurses. He'd told them he could not save their legs and he might not be able to save their lives (uncontrollable circumstances).

They'd then turned to walk back in the room to try and save these ladies lives. When they did, they saw that the two ladies had joined hands and were singing the song "You are Awesome in this Place, Mighty God" at the top of their lungs. Tears filled my eyes as I realized that even in the midst of uncontrollable circumstances, we can still declare how awesome God is!! Unfortunately, neither of the ladies lived. Very sad; however, I learned something from these two ladies that I never met on this earth . . . in the midst of all the hurt and heartache . . . GOD IS STILL AWESOME!!! Sometimes we have to praise Him from our pain, but praise Him anyway! He is truly awesome regardless of what we are going through today.

2) Problems brought on by ME

"A person's own folly leads to their ruin, yet their heart rages against the Lord." (Proverbs 19:3)

I want to be honest. I also want you to be honest. Sometimes we are going through seasons of chaos due to our own fault. OUCH!! It's true. I can look back on many times in my life that I ended up where I was because of my own bad choices and poor decisions. It wasn't anyone else's fault. I only have to look in the mirror. It is all on me.

The verse we just read in Proverbs always makes me go, "Hmmm."

Do you know people that continually make poor choices but also continually blame God for them? They get mad at God over their poor decisions. Well, okay, I am getting convicted just writing about this. HAHAHA!

Seriously though, we bring it on ourselves sometimes . . . some of us are "playing hurt" because of poor choices WE'VE made.

a) I know I am already in debt, but I sure want that new car.
b) I know that person is not a Christian but I can still date them; after all, I can lead them to the Lord.
c) I know my health is bad, but I can still eat what I want when I want. I think we all get the picture. Sometimes we just need to make better choices. Amen.

3) Other People

"With words of hatred they surround me; they attack me without cause." (Psalm 109:3)

Uh oh! It's true. Sometimes your peace is disrupted because of someone who has done you wrong. Maybe they lied about you or have intentionally tried to bring chaos to your life.

I recently saw a humorous meme with Kermit the Frog holding a phone and the caption said, "Hello, may I please speak with Jesus? I need help because these folks going to make me break at least four of the ten commandments." Hahahaha!

Funny but true.

We have all struggled with forgiving people that have tried to hurt us or even destroy us. While the Bible instructs us to forgive one another, let's be honest, it is very difficult. Our flesh always wants to rule in this situation. It disrupts our peace and keeps us in turmoil.

I will even reach a place where I feel like I have forgiven them. I am free from that person keeping me in turmoil. THEN I will see them or someone will mention their name. Uh Oh!! Then it all comes back to the surface. Let's be honest, it is an ongoing challenge. However, it is one we must meet and defeat. Confront it head on in prayer. Do not give anyone that much power over you. They are not your "peace giver," so don't let them be your "peace buster." Who knows, this might be the thing that heals your hurt.

4) War of Worry

"Anxiety weighs down the heart, but a kind word cheers it up." (Proverbs 12:25)

Worry robs us of our peace, and it can certainly weigh us down. If the enemy can keep us weighed down with worry, it will affect our peace. I don't know if you can relate to this, but I sure can . . .

"My mind is like my Internet browser . . . nineteen tabs are open . . . three of them are frozen, and I have no idea where the music is coming from." Hahaha!

I can definitely see that the enemy is targeting our minds. I have never prayed for so many Christians that are battling worry, depression, fears, etc. The enemy is working overtime to weigh us down with worry. Worry robs us of our peace.

If you put your head on the pillow at night to sleep, but you are worrying about something, it will rob you of your sleep. If you don't get rest, you will be physically tired. If we are physically tired, it makes us mentally and emotionally tired. If we are mentally and emotionally exhausted, it affects us spiritually. Do you see the devil's plan here? It all starts by controlling you with worry. I pray the weight of worry is lifting off of you right now. I pray you will sense God's peace even as you are reading this. Amen!

I recently saw this on social media: "Worry is a conversation you have with yourself about things you cannot change. Prayer is a conversation you have with God about things He CAN change." Please give it to God now. Worry, begone in Jesus' name! May the peace of God prevail over ALL the things you are worried about.

In closing this chapter, I want to take you back to the Haitian pastors' conference I spoke at . . .

Right before they introduced me, someone came up to me and said, "I just want to let you know that about 70 percent of these pastors here still don't know whether or not they will be able to eat tonight." They told me there were about four hundred pastors/spouses in attendance, and I was so taken back by that comment that I asked the gentleman to repeat it. He did. These spiritual leaders were attending this conference (many of them had walked several miles) and they still didn't know if they would have food to eat for their families that night. I confess I felt the weight of that while I preached.

After I finished preaching, I gave an altar call. Almost everyone came because the needs were great. I walked through the altars asking these leaders what I could pray with them about, and not one of them mentioned finances or food. Every single one of them wanted prayer for "lost family members" or "revival in their church." That's it. God moved in a powerful way that day, and I am grateful He used me to minister to those pastors. However, they ministered to me as well and never even knew it. I learned from those pastors that day that if we continue to seek first the Kingdom of God and His righteousness, everything in our lives will be taken care of. I have preached that all my life, but on that day, it came alive. I realized I was more worried than they were. They were all "playing hurt," but they were not going to let worry rob them from receiving from God. Will you?

I just want to close this chapter with these verses to encourage you in the Lord . . .

"Come to me all you who are weary and burdened, and I will give you rest." (Matt. 11:28)

"Peacemakers who sow in peace reap a harvest of righteousness." (James 3:18)

"Deceit fills hearts that are plotting evil; joy fills hearts that are planning peace." (Proverbs 12:20)

Discussion questions:

1) Discuss some things that might take away your peace.
2) How hard is it to accept that some things are simply out of our control?
3) Do you struggle with worry or anxiety?
4) Do you consider yourself a "peacemaker"? Why or why not?
5) Are "people" or "circumstances" the biggest "peace buster" in your walk with the Lord?

Chapter 9

UNFOCUSED VISION

WHEN WE USE THE WORD "VISION," WE CAN ACTUALLY GET TWO DIFFERENT interpretations of it:

1) I have sat in many leadership meetings (attendee) for both business and ministry. In those meetings, "vision casting" is often discussed. In other words, trying to SEE something before you actually SEE something.

The purpose of those discussions is to help us realize that it is not just about where we are but also about where we are going. "Where there is no vision, the people perish." (Proverbs 29:18). Where do you see yourself at this time next year? Where do you see yourself in five years? What are your action steps to get there? Those are the kind of questions asked when talking about "vision casting."

2) The other interpretation could be regarding our eyes. How well do you see? I need glasses, but not all the time. I can see fine at a distance; it's up close where I need help. So, when I read, I have to put on glasses. However, to see at a distance, I have to take them off. You may be like me or the opposite of me or you may be one who likes contacts. When we reach a "certain age," most of us need a little help with our vision. Glasses or contacts help us with our focus and clarity.

Why is vision so important? Why is it important to see things clearly? I really believe that HOW YOU VIEW THINGS WILL DETERMINE HOW YOU DO THINGS! If I can't see it OR see it clearly, then that might affect my action steps or lack thereof.

When we go to the eye doctor, we all are hoping for 20/20 vision. That seems to be the marker for "perfect" vision. I pray in the area of forgiveness; we can have a "spiritual" 20/20 vision. Let's learn from Joseph. In my opinion, he brings us one of the greatest examples of walking in forgiveness.

Josephs words were, "You intended to harm me, but God intended it for good to accomplish what is now being done, the saving of many lives." (Gen. 50:20)

Let's go back and take a look at how he arrived at a place to say those words. What a powerful place to arrive at! To be able to focus on God's intentions instead of the intentions of others. To remain focused on the intentions of others who are trying to harm you (or have tried) will mean an absence of peace in your life. A lack of forgiveness and wrong focus is a contributing factor to you "playing hurt."

In Genesis 37, Joseph was called a dreamer by his brothers and sold into slavery by them. I do want to point out here that Reuben was opposed to this. When talking about this story, we usually make it "all inclusive" with the brothers. That's not true. Reuben was opposed.

Let's continue the journey by hitting the highlights that will help us understand how Joseph arrived at 20/20 vision spiritually.

In Genesis 39, Potiphar purchased Joseph from the Ishmaelites, and he went to work for him. While working there, Potiphar's wife tried to seduce him . . . he refused her advances . . . she lied . . . Joseph ended up in prison. At this point, Joseph probably wasn't feeling like "his steps were ordered by the Lord." In Gen. 39:21, the Bible says, "While he was in prison, the Lord was with him."

Years passed and then Joseph interpreted Pharoah's dream. In gen. 41:41, we find that Pharoah put Joseph in charge of Egypt. In fact, he became second-in-command. I heard one preacher say, "He went from the pit to the palace." Now it feels more like the Lord is ordering our steps, right?

Just a few more highlights . . . a severe famine hit the land and Joseph's brothers were sent to Egypt to see if they could get some grain. They had to make their request to Joseph. Joseph recognized them, but they did not recognize him. He noticed Benjamin, his younger brother, was not with them, so he sent them back to get Benjamin. So, in Gen. 43, they made a second trip to Egypt. Joseph was very emotional, and I am sure he was fighting a lot of things in his mind as well.

Finally, in Genesis 45, Joseph made himself known to his brothers. It scared them. When his father, Jacob, passed away at the end of Gen. 49, his brothers got really scared then. In Gen. 50, they threw themselves at him and offered to be his slaves, but he refused by saying, "You intended to harm me, but God intended it for good to accomplish what is now being done, the saving of many lives." (Gen. 50:20). That's the "spiritual" 20/20 vision we are hoping to obtain. Seeing things that way will activate peace and cancel the chaos in our lives, even while "playing hurt."

Here is what I learned from this story . . .

1) ALWAYS DO THE RIGHT THING….

Joseph told his brothers, "You intended to harm me." He was right. They did intend to harm him. He wanted them to know that he knew that. However, he did not stoop to their level and try to retaliate.

Potiphar's wife lied about him in Gen. 39:13–15. She was angered because he repeatedly refused her advances and did not give in to her seductions.

So, with people whom he loved trying to harm him and other people lying about him . . . he kept doing the right thing. YOU NEVER GO WRONG BY DOING THE RIGHT THING!!

Several years ago, when I was living in Arkansas, I pulled through the drive-through at the bank. I made a deposit and requested some cash back from my check. I just laid it in the seat and drove about twenty miles to an appointment I had. I reached over and grabbed the cash before I walked in for my meeting. I noticed right away that something wasn't right. I counted it and realized that the bank teller had given me $200 too much.

My meeting lasted a couple of hours, so it was a while before I could get back to the bank. When I walked in, I saw the teller over in corner, trying to balance her drawer. She kept coming up $200 short, which would have been taken out of her pay. I called her over and told her that she had given me too much money back. She thanked me over and over again and was so relieved I'd brought it back.

Could I have used an extra $200? Absolutely. However, keeping that was simply the wrong thing to do. It was not mine, and I refused to let the enemy get one over on me. I firmly believe that if I would have kept that money, it would have eventually cost me way more than $200. Doing the right thing brings peace and avoids more hurt piling on in my life. I want to live in the peace that the Lord left.

2) PAIN CANNOT STEAL YOUR PROMISE . . .

The road to our promise usually includes pain. Joseph's pain included a trip to prison for something he didn't even do.

Jesus knew pain too. Judas betrayed him, Peter denied him, and his closest friends fell asleep on him when he needed them the most. Many of his followers went from HOSANNA to CRUCIFY HIM very quickly.

Don't let pain take away your dreams or rob you of your peace. It is part of the process, and it comes to teach us, not torment us. There are times we "play hurt," but it does not steal our promises from heaven.

3) **All pain has "teaching moments"** . . .

When Joseph's brothers were begging for their lives, he responded this way: "Don't be afraid, I am going to provide for both you and your children." (Gen. 50:21)

Learn from your pain, but don't lean on it. Let the Lord heal you because you don't want to bleed on people that did not cut you. Bitterness only adds to our pain in the long run. Don't let it lodge in your mind, heart, or spirit. Forgive and be reminded . . . sometimes you win, and sometimes you learn. Pain does have "teaching moments." Don't miss the lesson it teaches, or you are likely to repeat your mistakes.

4) **Our VICTORY TRUMPS THE POWER OF THE ENEMY'S WEAPON** . . .

(Isaiah 54:17) "no weapon formed against you will prevail . . ."

Joseph had 50/20 vision! His words in Gen. 50:20 were, ". . . to accomplish what is now being done." It all came full circle. His brothers put him in bondage, but God put him in charge!

Just because the weapon forms, does not mean that it will prosper. Dreams and visions still happen even though the weapon has formed. Live at peace knowing that Satan's weapons that have formed against you WILL NOT prosper or prevail in JESUS'S NAME!!!

You might be in a place in your life right now where all you can see are the weapons that have forms. It appears that circumstances, situations, or people have been assigned to ensure your demise. You have been hurt by the weapons before, and you can see that they are coming again. Let me encourage you to get your eyes off of the weapons and keep your eyes on the one who gives us victory! Jesus!! Don't lose faith; it may not look good right now, but know this... it ends good! You are a victor even in circumstances that were not your fault.

Discussion questions:

1) What are some of the weapons that the devil uses against us?
2) How do you respond when you are blamed for something you did not do?
3) Can you relate to Joseph's pain at all?
4) Do you often talk about and lean on the PROMISES of God?
5) Are you experiencing "spiritual fatigue" from the battle?

Chapter 10

THORNS AND THISTLES

ONE OF THE THINGS I AM OBSERVING IN THE WORLD TODAY (BOTH IN THE CHURCH AND outside) is an overwhelming presence of pain. It is glaringly evident that we are hurting mentally, physically, and emotionally. I am witnessing it in the churches I preach in as well as in my own family and among my own friends. I have the Lord for an increased healing anointing, and I challenge you to do the same.

In early June of 2022, the Lord gave me a vision. I am not quick to share these things publicly; in fact, I have only done it twice. I think the other times that I have had "defining moments" with God were more personal; however, on two different occasions, the Lord told me to share publicly. This is one of them. As a result of what I saw and what the Lord spoke to me, I began to preach a series called "Life Hurts BUT God heals!"

This is what the Lord showed me . . . I saw a huge crowd of people in a massive church setting. They were all worshipping the Lord with intensity. Praying and praising God at the top of their voices. It was intense! I then heard two words: "Look closely." So, I did, and I noticed that everyone was clothed in the FULL armor of God. Then I heard the words again, the same words, "Look closely." So, I did and noticed red streaks were coming out from underneath the armor. Everyone had red streaks. Everyone.

Then the Lord informed me that what I was seeing was the army of God praising God and pressing toward revival. It was intense. However, they were wounded underneath the armor, and the red I saw was them bleeding. Then the Lord spoke to me that the army of God is wounded and bleeding with all sorts of pain. We must concentrate on getting them healed. If the wounds are not treated and healed, they will become infected. Infection causes a lot of different problems in a lot of different ways.

Then the Lord took me to two verses:

"But I will restore your health and heal your wounds, declares the Lord" (Jeremiah 30:17)

"He heals the brokenhearted and binds up their wounds" (Psalm 147:3)

The picture of the blood running out from underneath the armor of God is something that will be forever embedded in my mind. I realized we can have on the armor of God and be ready for battle, but if we are wounded, it will greatly hinder us. It was at that moment I realized that it was time for the church to build a guardrail at the top of the cliff so we don't have to be an ambulance at the bottom of the cliff.

In Genesis 3:17–19 God is telling Adam what the price will be for his sin . . .

"To Adam he said, 'Because you listened to your wife and ate fruit from the tree about which I commanded you, 'You must not eat from it,'
Cursed is the ground because of you;
through painful toil you will eat food from it
all the days of your life.
It will produce thorns and thistles for you,
and you will eat the plants of the field.
By the sweat of your brow
you will eat your food
until you return to the ground,

since from it you were taken;
for dust you are
and to dust you will return.'"

In Verse 18, ONE of the things that God mentioned was "thorns and thistles." OUCH! I wish I could tell you that if you are a follower of Jesus Christ, there will never be pain, heartbreak, or heartache. I wish I could say that we will never experience loss or setbacks. The truth is, we do, and these verses are why.

Inflation, pandemics, lying, sickness and disease, and loss and division are at their highest levels in our current world. However, the deepest thorns for us are not what is going on in the world, but what is happening to us and to our friends and families.

Before we dive into this too deep, I want to mention that there is a difference between THORNS and FRUSTRATIONS:

It seems like every time I drop my toast in the morning, it falls on the side that I have already buttered. LOL!

It seems like the ONE tool I need is the one I cannot find. LOL!

I can find every other tool but the one I need.

When I pull up to the drive-through window at the bank and ALWAYS get in the shortest line, it ALWAYS turns out that the shortest line is also the slowest line. LOL!

Those are frustrations, not thorns. Frustrations can be humorous, thorns are not. We are talking about thorns. Let's look at what Scripture says . . .

First of all, the Bible talks about a CROWN OF THORNS. In John 19:2 it says, "The soldiers twisted together a crown of thorns and put it on his head . . ."

Let's focus on all that Christ went through on crucifixion day. He went through a beating and carried His own cross, spear in His side, nails in His hands and feet. He stood before Pilate as the people ridiculed Him and shouted, "Crucify, Crucify." He did it all with a CROWN OF THORNS piercing his head. He carried the curse of sin to the cross that day. He wore a crown of thorns so we could wear a crown in glory one day.

Did you ever feel like you were wearing a crown of thorns? Do you feel like something was constantly piercing you? It's always one thing and then another. Life hurts, BUT GOD HEALS! Playing hurt is not enjoyable ate all.

I also hear people say that if you are experiencing "thorns and thistles" of any kind, then something is wrong with you spiritually!!?? This makes no sense and is NOT Scriptural.

Romans 12:12 says, "Be joyful in hope, patient in affliction, and faithful in prayer."

Psalm 34:19 says, "The righteous person may have many troubles, but the Lord delivers him from them all."

Why would the Scripture tell us to be "patient in affliction" if we were not going to experience affliction? Why would Scripture tell us that the Lord will deliver us from trouble if we were not going to have trouble? The truth is we do have afflictions that equal thorns and thistles in our lives BUT God will deliver us from them all.

Secondly, let's talk about the EXEMPTION FROM THORNS. The truth is nobody is exempt. It does not matter how rich, how famous, or how holy you think you are, we all experience thorns and thistles. We hear stories every day of the rich and famous experiencing hurt and heartache. Nobody is exempt.

The Apostle Paul is a great example of this. He was the writer of two-third of the New Testament. After his conversion in Acts 9, he was a faithful servant of God. However, he reveals to us in 2 Cor. 12:7, ". . . therefore, in order to keep me from being conceited, I was given a thorn in my flesh, a messenger of Satan, to torment me." Paul had a THORN. He prayed about it. In fact, he sought God three times about it. He even shaved his head and undertook two different ten-day fasts.

The thorn was a constant pain for Paul, but God never removed it. He simply told Paul, "My grace is sufficient for you." (2 Corinthians 12:9)

"But he said to me, 'My grace is sufficient for you, for my power is made perfect in weakness.' Therefore, I will boast all the more gladly about my weaknesses, so that Christ's power may rest on me."

It may be the same for us. Thank God for His grace to make it through!

The third thing I want to talk about is the REMOVAL OF THORNS.

We have a promise that one day we will trade our crown of thorns (thorns and thistles) for a crown of glory!

"Do not be afraid of what you are about to suffer. I tell you; the devil will put some of you in prison to test you, and you will suffer persecution for ten days. Be faithful, even to the point of death, and I will give you life as your victor's crown." (Rev. 2:10)

Be faithful. Stand firm. Keep fighting. The day is coming when all hurt, heartache, and pain will be wiped away. The day is coming when we will receive a crown of life, and we will forever be with the Lord!

I love what Paul said when he knew his life was about to end . . .

"I have fought a good fight, I finished the race, and I have kept the faith. Now there is in store for me a crown of righteousness, which the Lord, the righteous judge, will award to me on that day—not to me only, but to all those who long for His appearing." (2 Timothy 4:7–8)

In all of our suffering and dealing with the thorns and thistles, will you hold on to the crown of righteousness just like Paul did?

In May, 2022, we celebrated forty years of full-time ministry. My board of directors had a celebration banquet in our honor. It was humbling to see many friends and family members gather to celebrate with us. It was truly a night we will never forget.

That evening my board of directors received an offering for us and sent us on a very nice vacation to the northeastern part of the United States. It was a "bucket list" trip for us. Dianna and I are both really into history, and that area of our country is loaded with it. We went to five different states in ten days, and it was so much fun. I will always be grateful for that trip that was made possible by our friends and family.

The last two days we spent in Boston. We stayed in the downtown area, and even though we had a rented car, we opted to take an Uber everywhere we went. I am not much for driving in big cities that are unfamiliar to me. The last day we were heading back to the motel. We were going to get packed up because we had a flight back home the next morning.

In downtown Boston, there are several places where you cross the street to get to a concrete island and then you have to cross another street to get to the other side. We were sitting in the back seat of our Uber and it was raining outside. All of the sudden we saw a couple of young girls running, laughing, and jumping puddles. They were having fun playing in the rain. They crossed the street in front of us, but instead of waiting on the island for traffic to stop on the other street, they kept going. They were continuing to laugh and jump puddles as they ran. The first girl made it across just fine, but the second girl was hit by a car. Dianna and I watched as her body went flying in the air and landed in the street. It appeared to clip her and not hit her head-on, so the injuries did not look life-threatening but she was in horrible pain while lying in the street.

The driver stopped and got out of the car, her friend came back to just hold her, and people were rushing to see if they could help. We just sat in the car and cried. We felt helpless. Since I have a daughter, Karissa, I immediately felt an urge to hug her. I also thought of this girl's father. We prayed because that's all we could do. She was hurting, and we were helpless.

The reality is that there was nothing we could do to stop her pain. We could only pray. We all are experiencing thorns and thistles of our own, but we are also watching others deal with their own hurts and heartaches. We feel helpless. All we can do is pray . . . so . . . we pray.

Thorns and thistles cause an absence of peace in our lives. Sometimes it is for long periods of time too. It is hard to have peace with the thorns of life sticking into you constantly. Thorns and thistles are a confirmation we are "playing hurt," but HIS GRACE IS SUFFICIENT FOR US!!

Discussion questions:

1) What are some things that constantly stick into you like a thorn?
2) How do you spiritually fight through the pain?
3) Do you have any open wounds that need to be cleaned out and healed before they get infected?
4) Do you realize that your pain is not a signal that something is wrong in your relationship with God?
5) Can you identify people in your circle who are hurting right now? Are you aware of their pain?

Chapter 11

BY HIS STRIPES

WHEN THE PANDEMIC HIT OUR COUNTRY, SICKNESS AND DISEASE BECAME THE headlines for months, now turning into years. Honestly, I have never seen so many people under attack physically. I have never heard of sickness and disease dominating so many lives as they are right now. When we get a bad report from the doctor, it paralyzes our life in every way. Our emotions go all over the map, and everything else must take second place so that we can focus on getting well. This definitely can fall into the category of a "peace buster."

I want us to look at two different portions of Scripture before we go any further. One is in the Old Testament, and the other is in the New Testament.

"To this you were called, because Christ suffered for you, leaving you an example that you should follow in His steps.

He committed no sin, and no deceit was found in His mouth.

When they hurled their insults at Him, He did not retaliate; when He suffered, He made no threats. Instead, He entrusted Himself to Him who judges justly. He Himself bore our sins in His body on the cross, so that we might die to sins and live for righteousness; "by His wounds you have been healed." For "you were like sheep going astray," but now you have returned to the Shepherd and overseer of your souls." (1 Peter 2:21–25)

"Surely, He took up our pain and bore our suffering, yet we considered Him punished by God, stricken by Him, and afflicted.

But He was wounded for our transgressions, He was crushed for our iniquities; the punishment that brought us peace was on Him, and by His wounds we are healed." (Isaiah 53:4–5)

I gave you these two portions of Scripture back-to-back for a purpose. I wanted you to see that the benefits of the atonement include both spiritual and physical healing. The Lord Jesus Christ gave His life on a cross for us. These verses tell us that we receive both the benefit of salvation and physical healing because He willingly laid down His life for us.

Peter talked about the fact that Christ "bore our sins in His body on the cross, so that we might die to sins and live for righteousness." (1 Peter 2:24). It always amazes me when I think about the depth of this. Jesus died for our sins before He even knew if we would choose to accept what He did for us. In other words, He gave His life in hope that we would take advantage of the benefit of salvation. He had no guarantee we would. Since we are free moral agents, we decide for ourselves. So, the fact that He gave His life just so that all of mankind would have the option, well, that humbles me beyond words. THANK YOU, JESUS!!

Isaiah talked about the physical healing that is available to us because of the thirty-nine stripes Jesus took on His back. He did not have to do that. He was already going to the cross to die for our sins. That would have been enough. However, they took off His robe, and a soldier laid thirty-nine stripes across His back. He could have called for the angels to get Him out of it, but He stood there and took a severe beating. Why would He do that? I believe Jesus had the ability to see through time and know that sickness and disease would rack our bodies. He wanted authors to be able to write and preachers to be able to preach that BY THOSE STRIPES WE WERE HEALED!!!!

So, you see, both spiritual and physical healing are included in the atonement. If you are reading this right now and you are sick in your body, then I declare healing and health over you right now in the name of JESUS!

I hope this isn't a morbid illustration for you because I am just sharing facts. The Bible tells us that (if the Lord tarries) we all have an appointment with death. IF I die of sickness or disease, I want the preacher at my funeral to say at some point in their message, "GOD IS A HEALER." That's right. I also hope there are a lot of "AMENS" to this declaration! Why do I want this? The reason is because many people will struggle with God not healing me, and I want it known that God is a healer whether He heals me or not. God is a healer whether He heals you or not. God IS a healer because the Word of God says HE IS A HEALER!! That does not change just because He did not heal me.

Exodus 15:26 says, "I am the Lord who heals you!"

Psalm 103:3 says, ". . . He heals all of our diseases"

Exodus 23:25 says, "Worship the Lord your God, and His blessings will be on your food and water. I will take away sickness from among you."

He is a healer whether He heals us or not. He is a healer because the Bible says He is a healer. I will keep praying because it is what the Bible tells me to do. In other words, I will do my part, and let the Lord take it from there. That is also Scriptural . . .

"Is anyone among you sick? Let them call the elders of the church to pray over them and anoint them with oil in the name of the Lord.

The prayer offered in faith will make the sick person well; the Lord will raise them up. If they have sinned, they will be forgiven." (James 5:14–15)

Jehovah Rapha . . . the GOD WHO HEALS!!!

Please consider the following:

- Five times in the Old Testament, God healed barren women
- Four times He healed plagues that were brought on by sin
- He healed Moses, Miriam, and Naaman the leper
- Three times He raised people from the dead
- There are six other accounts of healing, two of them of thousands of people at once

TOTAL: Sixteen individual healings, seven mass healings, and twenty-three other accounts of people being healed.

God healed before Jesus ever got to earth. The Old Testament bears that out. Then in the New Testament, we see Jesus Himself healing the sick on a number of occasions. We see the disciples, Paul and others, praying for the sick, and they are healed. Keep praying for people, and keep believing in our healing as well.

I want to give you what I call a "Biblical Framework for Healing" . . .

1) God is sovereign . . .

God decides who is healed on earth. If it was up to me, everyone would be healed and healed immediately.

Only eternity will reveal why some are healed and some are not. Please believe me, I have tried to figure this out. I have researched this in God's Word, trying to find the answer to the question, "Why are some people I pray for healed immediately while others are never healed?" Why? Honestly, I don't know. I have to leave it to the sovereignty of God.

I've asked this question already, but it bears repeating here, "Why did God send an angel and let Peter out of prison, but He left John the Baptist in prison and he got his head cut off?" WHY? Could God have sent an angel and had John the Baptist released too? YES!!! Did God love Peter more than He loved John the Baptist? NO!! That is crazy! God loves all of us the same. So why then?

There are times we must get to the place where Duet. 29:29 is released in our spirits: "The secret things belong to God, and the things that are revealed belong to us." We just have to leave it to God and His infinite wisdom.

If you are experiencing grief today over someone you have lost, please remember that HEAVEN IS HEALING TOO! They did experience healing, just not the way we would have preferred. We would prefer not to be separated from our friends and family when they experience their healing. I lost both of my parents to disease, so I do find "some" comfort in that. I pray you do as well.

2) God commissions us to pray for the sick . . .

When we pray for the sick, it is an act of obedience to God. In Luke 10:9, the twelve disciples and seventy others were told to "heal the sick."

Then as a part of the GREAT COMMISSION in Mark 16:15–18, Jesus said in Verse 18 for us to lay our hands on sick people and they will get well. We are commissioned to pray for the sick.

I have such a burden for this that I have prayed that God would give me a healing anointing. I pray for it not only during church services but everywhere I go. I want you to know that this anointing is not just accessible to those of us in full time ministry. It is available to every child of God. Would you ask God for that anointing as well? An anointing that you could lay hands on the sick and they would recover? I pray that you will have the faith to walk into your sick child's bedroom when they are sick and lay hands on them, pray the prayer of faith, and see them healed! I pray you have the faith the pray over a sick coworker or someone you randomly meet and see them healed in Jesus's name! God commissioned it, so let's do it.

3) Compassion is the motive to pray for the sick . . .

1 Cor. 12:28 says, there are "gifts of healings." I am praying for the gift, but I am still most affected with compassion. Jesus had compassion for the sick. It truly moved Him. Does it move us?

If we ask the Lord to break our hearts for the things that break His heart, then our hearts would be broken for the sick.

As I walk through the altar area of churches to pray for the sick, I usually ask them what I can pray with them about. I do this so that I can pray specifically. The requests are heartbreaking, and I am truly moved with compassion for them. I do not know them or their story; however, I am genuinely compassionate toward them. That is why I pray fervently for the Lord to intervene and bring healing to their bodies.

4) God responds to faith

Hebrews 11:6 says, "Without faith it is impossible to please God."

God is moved by our faith. Faith attracts God. I always want to pray in FAITH that God will heal the sick.

Would you pause from reading this right now and ask God to give you a "faith lift?" Please ask God to cancel doubt from your life and give you an anointing to heal the sick. We cannot do it without Him. HE IS THE HEALER!!

It has been more than a decade now, but we have experienced a supernatural healing in our family . . .

I have already shared the first part of this story, but I must repeat a portion of it because it all flows together with our testimony. I was preaching a revival meeting in Enid, OK, for my longtime friends, Pastors Kevin and

Tami Ward. I was in Kevin's office on Wednesday afternoon, and we were just talking about the final night of the revival. My cell phone rang a couple of times, but it was from a number I did not recognize. (I am not sure who "spam risk" is, but I wish they would quit calling me.) I don't typically answer if I don't recognize the number. Kevin and I finished our conversation, and I left his office, got in my car, and the same number called me again. This time I answered it. The call came from Kevin Egly, who was one of my father-in-law's board members at the church he was pastoring in in Bixby, OK. He said, "Lynn, Ken and Freda (my in-laws) have been in a car accident, and Freda did not survive." My heart broke, and I felt a strong pulling to get to my wife, who was not with me on the road.

I went back into Pastor Kevin's office. He was consoling me at the same time he was trying to help me make phone calls and preparations to leave immediately to be with my wife. The accident had happened on Interstate 40 in Ozark, AR, so they had taken my father-in-law, who walked away with a chipped tooth, to a local church there.

Dianna and I were living in Conway, AR, at that time, and so I contacted our pastors, Randy and Patty Long, and asked them if they would go tell my wife that her mom had passed away. It would be a few hours before I could arrive, and I did not want Dianna to be alone when she heard the news.

Let me rewind the story for just a moment . . . My in-laws had come to visit us while I was out of town preaching because my wife had a doctor's appointment. Since I wasn't going to be there to go with her, they'd come to visit so my mother-in-law could go to the appointment with Dianna. They'd left right after the appointment, and the accident had happened on the Interstate while they were on their way home.

Our pastors ended up bringing Dianna to the church where her dad was. Dianna's sister was there as well. Pastor Kevin Ward drove me to Oklahoma City where my brother, Dennis, picked me up and drove me to meet everyone else at the church in Ozark, AR. Since it was about a four-hour drive,

I spent a lot of time on the phone fielding questions and concerns from friends and family members. It seemed like a VERY long four hours. I wanted to get to my wife.

We finally made it. I greeted my wife, father-in-law, and others that had come to pay their respects. After I had been there a few minutes, Dianna said she needed to talk to me privately. We walked out to the church's parking lot so we could have a private conversation. She informed me that just a few minutes after she was told that her mom had passed away, the doctor's office had called saying they'd found a mass in her lower stomach. WHAT??!!

My heart sank, and my mind began to spin. The word "mass" never sounds good. Dianna told me that she would prefer to keep this between us until after the funeral. She was obviously concerned about her dad and wanted to make sure that we were there for him.

We ended up staying in Tulsa for two weeks. I preached at the funeral, and it was truly a blessing to see so many friends and family members honor my mother-in-law, Freda Linn. However, it was also very hard. We were PLAYING HURT for sure.

We finally felt like we'd got to a place that we could go back home. We went home and got back in our routine. I started traveling again, and things returned to the best level of "normal" that we could get to after all that. About a month later I came in from preaching at a meeting, and Dianna told me she was ready to go back to the doctor and find out what they had found. This time the appointment was scheduled when I could be with her.

The day of the appointment came, and we were called back to the room where we would see the doctor. They put Dianna up on the patients' table, and I sat in a chair in the corner of the room. I was actually able to see the X-ray from where I was sitting, and I could even see the mass. The nurse came in and informed us that since it had been several weeks since Dianna had last come in, they needed to take another X-ray for the doctor to look at. They were running a medical device across Dianna's stomach so they could find the mass. I think they wanted to see if it had grown. However, the nurse could not find it. I could see what was happening, but Dianna couldn't because she was lying on the table. I was trying to contain myself so I didn't scare or embarrass my introverted wife. The nurse even asked her why she'd come back in. We told her what we had been through and why it had taken us so long to come back. The nurse then told Dianna what I could already see: "The mass is gone." She told us she would show the doctor the X-ray, and she left the room. In less than five minutes she came back and told us we were free to go; the doctor did not even need to see her. Praise the Lord!!

We will always KNOW in our hearts that God healed Dianna. The mass was there, and then it was gone. In the middle of a lot of tragedy, hurt, and heartache for our family . . . God showed Himself as a healer of Dianna's body. She has never had another problem. God is good.

Preachers keep preaching that our God heals!!
Believers keep praying for the sick to be healed!!
Let's all keep the faith and leave the rest to God!!

Life hurts BUT God heals!! Keep pressing through your pain. Keep the faith. Miracles will manifest!!

God is our peace in the middle of tragedy and bad reports. Thank you, Lord!

Discussion questions:

1) Have you ever been physically healed?
2) Have you ever witnessed a physical healing in someone else?
3) Why don't we see more of this is our church services?
4) Do you struggle with God's sovereignty?
5) Are you willing to commit to praying for the sick yourself, regardless of where you are?

CHAPTER 12

PURSUIT OF REVIVAL

DO YOU FEEL SPIRITUALLY COLD? DO YOU NEED THE FIRE OF GOD TO BURN IN YOUR heart and life again? Do you need a FRESH TOUCH from our heavenly Father? Are you feeling spiritually dry and barren? We have all been there during different seasons in our lives. We have all experienced those times where it seemed like God was a long way from us. In fact, He was so far away that we couldn't hear His voice or feel His touch. It is in those seasons that we seem to experience confusion, doubt, and chaos at a new level. After all, we know that God is always near us. We know that He will never leave us or forsake us. However, we sure don't feel Him.

I have heard it said in many different ways, but I think my favorite is this: "If you don't feel as close to God as you used to, guess who moved?" We know the answer, right? So, if we don't feel as close to Him as we used to, let's do whatever it takes to get back to Him. Remember, it is not a "feeling" walk, it is a "faith" walk.

The Psalmist experienced this and prayed this prayer,

"You, Lord, showed favor to your land; you restored the fortunes of Jacob. You forgave the iniquity of your people and covered all their sins. You set aside all your wrath and turned from your fierce anger. Restore us again, God our Savior, and put away your displeasure toward us. Will you be angry with us forever? Will you prolong your anger through all generations? Will you not revive us again, that your people may rejoice in you? Show us your unfailing love, Lord, and grant us your salvation." (Psalm 85:1–7)

The two things that stick out to me in this prayer are:

1) 'Restore us again" (V. 4)
2) "Revive us again" (V. 6)

The secret to both personal and worldwide revival is very clear in Scripture . . . PRAY!!

"If my people, who are called by my name, will humble themselves and pray and seek my face and turn from their wicked ways, then I will hear from heaven, and I will forgive their sin and heal their land." (2 Chronicles 7:14)

I know that if you believe the Bible, then you believe that verse. IF we pray, we will heal from heaven, and our land will be healed. We believe that. However, please know that if you believe that verse, then you must also believe that its opposite is true as well. If we do NOT pray, we will NOT hear from heaven, and our land will NOT be healed. It sounds to me like it is up to us. I encourage you to pray. Let's do our part, and I believe God will do His.

In 1857 there was a forty-six-year-old man named Jeremiah Lanphier who lived in New York City. Jeremiah loved the Lord with all of his heart, but he could never seem to find his place. He wanted God to use him, but he just didn't know how. He was beyond excited when one day he got an invitation from his church leadership to come on staff as "inner city missionary." Jeremiah had a great burden for the lost, so he felt like this was the way God was finally going to use him.[2]

---

2 "America's Great Revivals, Bethany House Publishers, Minneapolis, MN. 2004"

So, in July of 1857 he started walking up and down the streets of New York City passing out tracts and talking to people about Jesus. However, he did it all without success. Jeremiah sought the Lord about what he might do differently, and the Lord put prayer in his heart.

So, Jeremiah printed up a bunch of posters and tracts and began to pass them out to anyone and everyone he met. He invited anyone who wanted to come to the third floor of the Old North Dutch Reform Church on Fulton St. in New York City from 12 to 1 p.m. on Wednesday to pray. He literally passed out hundreds and hundreds of fliers and put-up hundreds of posters. Wednesday came and at noon, nobody showed up. So, Jeremiah got down on his knees and starting praying alone. For two weeks, he prayed alone because nobody showed up. The third week he, once again, began to pray by himself. He'd prayed alone for thirty minutes when at 12:30 five other people walked in and began to pray with him. The next week twenty people came. The next week between thirty and forty people came.

They then decided to meet every day from noon to 1 p.m. to pray for the city. It wasn't long until other ministers started joining and said, "We need to start this in our churches." Within six months, there were over five thousand prayer groups meeting every day in New York. Soon the word spread all over the country. Prayer meetings were started in Philadelphia, Detroit, and Washington, DC. In fact, President Franklin Pierce started going almost every day to a noon prayer meeting.

By 1859 some fifteen thousand churches in America were having prayer meetings every day at noon and thousands were brought to Christ.[3]

The thing I love most about this revival is that it was not started in a megachurch by a famous preacher. It was started by one man who began to pray. One man who said I will show up even if nobody else does. One man who said I will pray even if nobody else prays.

---

3 "Revival Born in a Prayer Meeting", www.cslewisinstitute.org"

I believe God is still looking for one man or one woman or one student who will say the same. Is that you? Will you pray if nobody else prays? I challenge you to keep praying through your pain. Keep praying through your chaos. Prayer is not preparation for the battle; prayer IS the battle. Win the battle in prayer. Live in personal revival. It helps us deal with the hurts and heartaches we experience.

At the time of this writing, I have been an evangelist (traveling minister) for thirty-six years. In those thirty-six years I have said one phrase everywhere I have been. In fact, I have repeated it multiple times in the same churches. Even though I say it frequently, I realize it has never been as true as it is right now.

That phrase is, "Our world needs revival."

Before I continue this chapter, I feel like I need to stop and define revival. I am sure as a follower of Jesus Christ, you, like me, immediately get something in your mind when someone says the word "revival." Since I grew up in church, I automatically go to this definition, "We are bringing in a guest preacher, and we are going to church consecutive nights for a week." That is what "revival" was to me growing up and for most of my adult life.

I decided to go to Webster's dictionary to see how it defines revival. I found multiple definitions, and most of them were connected to the medical field. Someone was dead and they were revived. However, that wasn't really what I was looking for. I kept reading and finally found one definition that resonated deep in heart. One definition said, "An improvement in the condition or strength of something." BOOM! That's it! Revival is continuing to be better than you were the day before. It is striving daily to be spiritually stronger. It is committing that every time I leave a church service, I will be better than when I came. Striving to be better helps us work through the trials we face and the hurts we experience.

The word "revive" is mentioned sixteen times in Scripture. Fourteen out of the sixteen are in the Old Testament. In Scripture it not only means to live and have life but also to remain alive. To sustain life. May our pursuit of revival prevail over our pain. May revival quicken us from sickness, discouragement, and faintheartedness.

PROCESS OF REVIVAL . . .

I have discovered that there is a process we must go through to arrive at that place of revival.

1) REVIVAL STARTS WITH ME!

"Create in ME a pure heart, O God, and renew a steadfast spirt in ME." (Psalm 51:10)

"Woe is ME!" I cried. "I am ruined! I am a man of unclean lips . . ." (Isaiah 6:5) (Emphasis provided by author)

We are all in different places in our walk with God. We are all experiencing different hurts and pains. Some of us need our faith revived, while others need a reviving of passion, integrity, marriage, career, finances, emotions, focus, etc. We are all in different places with different needs, BUT it is the SAME God who is our answer! Wherever you are at and whatever it is that you need, pray right now that God would start a revival in YOU right where you are. I have found over and over again that God will meet us where we are and take us to where He wants us to be.

2) It then moves to US . . .

PERSONAL REVIVAL LEADS TO WORLDWIDE REVIVAL

It goes from me to us! If individuals experience it, it will spread to our families and our churches and our towns and our world. Grant it oh God!!!

"Will you not revive US again, that your people may rejoice in you? (Psalm 85:6)

"Then we will not turn away from you; revive US, and we will call on your name" (Psalm 80:18)

It is a process. Let revival start with me and spread to others.

I want to take us back now to the first verses I shared in this chapter. There is something very important that I don't want you to miss. The prayer in Psalm 85 shows us two things: God has done it before, and God will do it again!

Let's look again at the first three verses of the prayer:

"You, Lord, showed favor to your land; you restored the fortunes of Jacob. You forgave the iniquity of your people and covered all their sins. You set aside all your wrath and turned from your fierce anger." (Psalm 85:1–3)

Please notice the following words in those verses . . . showed, restored, forgave, covered, and turned. All of these words are framed in the past tense. He started his prayer by acknowledging what God had ALREADY done. He was giving God thanks for PAST provisions and miracles. He hasn't prayed yet for revival or restoration; he spent the first three verses saying THANK YOU LORD for what you have already done.

I confess that I have been guilty of these many times. I forget to say "Thank you Lord for what you have ALREADY done for me." I often get caught up in "asking God" and forget to thank him for what He has already done. God has been good to us already. I often say, "If God doesn't do another thing for me, He has been good to me." Please take a minute right now and say THANK YOU Lord for what you have already done for me. He is a good, good Father!

Lynn Wheeler

As I am writing this today, my mind goes back to the many miracles that God has done over the last forty years of my ministry. As I reflect, I rejoice. God has done it before, and I want to share just one miracle that happened several years ago . . .

I was invited to preach at a Sunday-Wednesday revival meeting in the town of Grandy, NC. I had been to this church several times and so I knew the pastor and a few of the people well. I got up to preach on Sunday morning, and I must say it was difficult to preach that morning. I sensed that the enemy was working hard in that service. He did not want the Word being preached.

I recall having a five-point message that morning, and after preaching my introduction and first point, I stopped. I sensed such a heaviness in the church that morning that I told them we were going to stop and pray before I continued. I wanted whatever was hindering that service to be broken in Jesus's name! I had the church bow their heads and close their eyes, and we all began to pray. I had come off the church platform and into the altar area while I was praying. I was pacing back and forth across the altar area while asking God to lift the depression and give us a breakthrough so we could finish that service with liberty and freedom.

As I was pacing and praying, all of a sudden, I felt something hit me in the shoulder. It startled me. I looked up and saw that someone had thrown something at me. I noticed that a bottle of pills had hit me and rolled up under the first row of chairs in the sanctuary. I walked over and picked it and read the prescription. Now, I am not a doctor and I do not play one on TV, but I recognized the medication. I recognized it only because I had seen a commercial about it on television. It was medication for depression. I raised the bottle and said, "Who just threw these at me?" Well, most of the people were surprised because they had their heads bowed and eyes closed. They were praying so they hadn't seen what had happened. Well, the only people that had were the "peekers." Some of you all are peeking and praying.

Almost immediately a lady stood up who was sitting on the back row of the church. She had tears streaming down her face, and she said, "It was me, Preacher." She went on, "I do not even go to church here. I am in town visiting my sister." Her sister had bowed her head in embarrassment. Then she said, "When you were praying, it dawned on me that I had been on that medication more than half of my life. I got so frustrated that I just reached in my purse, grabbed those pills, and slung them. I didn't mean to hit you, Preacher."

I called her to the front of the church and asked some ladies to come and pray for her. There were about a dozen ladies praying and crying as this precious sister in the Lord called out to God for help. I just left them praying and went on and finished my sermon. I preached the rest of that message with such freedom and God moved in a powerful way that morning. In fact, that week ended up being so powerful that the pastor and I agreed this revival should go another week. To make a long story short, that revival meeting ended up lasting five weeks. In five weeks, 201 people gave their hearts to the Lord. It was a powerful time of people pursuing God.

During the third week of revival, the lady, who had gone back home, sent an email to her sister. The pastor had her get up and read it to the church. In essence, she'd said that she had gone to her doctor and after some testing, he'd taken her off of her medication. Praise the Lord!! That revival broke out, and depression was lifted when one person got set free in her mind. It took one miracle for one person to set that in motion. That is just one story of the many testimonies I have that GOD HAS DONE IT BEFORE!!

If He has done it before, He will do it again! The prayer continued in Psalm 85, after the psalmist gave thanks for past victories, THEN he cried out for revival and restoration.

"Restore us again" (V. 4)
"Revive us again" (V. 6)

I declare over you today that, even in the middle of all of your heartache, God is restoring you! He is reviving you too! You are "playing hurt," but the chaos is replaced by the peace of God. God's presence prevails over our pain! Amen!!

Discussion questions:

1) What does the phrase "revival starts with me" mean?
2) How can we move from "me" to "us" as far as revival goes?
3) Do you ever pray for revival? Why or why not?
4) What does the term "revival" mean to you?
5) Describe some great revival experiences you may have experienced.

CHAPTER 13

BECAUSE OF MY DADDY

I HAVE NO DOUBT THAT A LOT OF PEOPLE ARE STRUGGLING IN THIS AREA. I SEE IT WAY more often than I want to. Open wounds from pain inflicted by family members. Maybe you were deserted or neglected or abused by your family, and those wounds have never been healed. Perhaps you never talked about or even prayed about it. Or maybe you have been to counseling multiple times to try to deal with that pain. Either way, I am sorry you are hurting. I am sorry for what you have been through. We cannot undo what has been done, but we can pursue, with the help of the Lord, healing from the pain.

I will be talking about marriage in a different chapter, so I want to specifically talk about mothers, fathers, and children in this chapter. Whether it was in your past and how you grew up or it is a current situation that makes your home life very difficult, God is our answer. Either way, He is our healer! Let's start with these verses:

Matthew 4:18–22 . . . "18 As Jesus was walking beside the Sea of Galilee, he saw two brothers, Simon, called Peter, and his brother Andrew. They were casting a net into the lake, for they were fishermen. 19 'Come, follow me,' Jesus said, 'and I will send you out to fish for people.' 20 At once they left their nets and followed him.

21 Going on from there, he saw two other brothers, James, son of Zebedee, and his brother John. They were in a boat with their father Zebedee,

preparing their nets. Jesus called them, 22 and immediately they left the boat and their father and followed him."

When I am thinking about families, and I read those verses, I must admit it brings some immediate questions to my mind.

Why didn't Zebedee go? Did Jesus not call him? Was his work or business more important than following Jesus? I mean Verse 22 says, "Immediately they left the boat and their father and followed Him." Then later in Matt. 20:20 we find that their mother was following Christ but we never read in Scripture that Zebedee ever did. Everybody followed, that is, everybody BUT daddy. Hmmmm???

Let's take a pause from this teaching time and look at something dads are very famous for: DAD JOKES!!! I just had a vision of my kids rolling their eyes. You know I have to share a few, and so before I do, let me go ahead and say, you're welcome.

A young father walked the hallways of the hospital all night long while his wife was in labor, wringing his hands and sweating bullets all night long. Finally, the nurse came out about 4 a.m. and said, "Congratulations, it is a girl." The young father immediately replied, "OH THANK GOD, that means she will never have to go through what I went through tonight." Uh oh. I somehow feel like I need to apologize to all the moms right now.

It is interesting that the word "father" appears in the dictionary right before the word "fatigued" and right after the word "fathead."

Ok. I am done and once again, YOU ARE WELCOME!

The truth is that Mother's Day is a big deal, and it should be.

Father's Day, not so much.

A five-year-old boy was asked what Father's Day meant to him. His reply was, "It's the same as Mother's Day except the presents cost less." I know that I speak for all fathers when I say we don't mind. I will make sure Mom's gift always costs more. I love to bless and celebrate the ladies for all the things they do for our families.

Many of you have parents that are still alive, and you get to celebrate them often. Yet, there are many, like me, who have lost their parents already. Some have fond memories; others, not so much. Some have experienced the pain from a father who was absent or never cared. Some know the pain of having hateful, critical words spoken over them by a father. If that is you, I CANCEL those words off of your life right now in the name of Jesus! Life hurts, BUT God heals. Our heavenly Father can heal any wound you have.

Next, I want to look at two different fathers in Scripture:

1) **Issacs's Father, Abraham**

    I see three characteristics here in Genesis 26 . . .

    a) **He Obeyed . . .**

    Genesis 26:1–6: "Now there was a famine in the land—besides the previous famine in Abraham's time—and Isaac went to Abimelech king of the Philistines, in Gerar. The Lord appeared to Isaac and said, 'Do not go down to Egypt; live in the land where I tell you to live. Stay in this land for a while, and I will be with you and will bless you. For to you and your descendants I will give all these lands and will confirm the oath I swore to your father Abraham. I will make your descendants as numerous as the stars in the sky and will give them all these lands, and through your offspring all nations on earth will be blessed because Abraham obeyed me and did everything I required of him, keeping my commands, my decrees, and my instructions.' So, Isaac stayed in Gerar."

All of the land that was given and the generational blessings that were obtained came down to one act of obedience. "Because Abraham obeyed me and did everything, I required of him . . ."

May every person reading this right now (not just the fathers) strive to obey God and His commands above all else.

b) Contended . . .

Gen. 26:12–15, "Isaac planted crops in that land and the same year reaped a hundredfold, because the Lord blessed him. 13 The man became rich, and his wealth continued to grow until he became very wealthy. 14 He had so many flocks and herds and servants that the Philistines envied him. 15 So all the wells that his father's servants had dug in the time of his father Abraham, the Philistines stopped up, filling them with earth."

Contend for your faith! Let's undo what the devil has done in our families. We CAN take back what the enemy has stolen.

c) Praised . . .

Gen. 26:23–25, "From there he went up to Beersheba. (24) That night the Lord appeared to him and said, 'I am the God of your father Abraham. Do not be afraid, for I am with you; I will bless you and will increase the number of your descendants for the sake of my servant Abraham.'

(25) Isaac built an altar there and called on the name of the Lord. There he pitched his tent, and there his servants dug a well."

Isaac was reminded that, "I am the God of your father Abraham." (vs. 24) Then God declared blessings over him in every way, including an increase in the number of his descendants. Isaac's response was to go and build an altar and give praise to his God and the God of his father. Don't forget to give praise for all he has done and is doing in your life. He is worthy of all the praise and glory we can give to Him!

In 1980, while I was a sophomore in college, our entire dorm gathered in the TV room at the end of the hall to watch a hockey game. It was the Olympics and the United States were playing Russia in the Lake Placid winter games. Jim Craig was the goalie for the USA, and that night he stopped thirty-six out of thirty-nine shots on goal. The USA won that night, and it is still considered one of the greatest upsets in sports. Two days later we beat Finland 4-2 for the gold medal. While everyone was celebrating the victory, Jim Craig wrapped a flag around himself and began to skate across the ice. The camera followed him, and you could read his lips as he looked in the stands, He was asking, "Where is my father?" He wanted to celebrate with his father.

My father has gone on to be with the Lord. I will never forget the night he led me to the Lord. I was six years old when he prayed with me at an altar, and it is still a very clear memory to me. When I get to heaven, I will probably ask the same question, "Where is my father?" I hope my kids do the same. Will yours?

The next father I want to talk about is…..

Mephibosheth's Father

David was now the king, and he decided he wanted to show kindness to a descendant of his friend Jonathan and Jonathan's father Saul. He'd heard about a young man named Mephibosheth, and so he had him brought to him.

2 Samuel 9:7–8, "Don't be afraid," David said to him, "for I will surely show you kindness for the sake of your father Jonathan. I will restore to you all

the land that belonged to your grandfather Saul, and you will always eat at my table."

(8) Mephibosheth bowed down and said, "What is your servant, that you should notice a dead dog like me?"

His father and grandfather had both been killed in the same battle. In an effort to get him to safety, his caregiver had dropped him when he was five years old. It was such a hard fall that it had crippled Mephibosheth in both feet. Since then, he had been living in LoDebar. King David had summoned him to tell him he was restoring his grandfather's and father's land to him AND that he and his son, Mica, would always eat at the king's table. David did not know him or even about him. He did all this BECAUSE OF HIS DADDY!

His daddy or his grandpa couldn't change the fact that he was crippled in both feet, but they helped change his economic status even though they were no longer alive: a positive generational effect from a father and grandfather that he probably barely remembered.

I pray that I can be such a father.

One of our faithful ministry partners is extra special to me. She has supported our ministry monthly for several years. In fact, she is one of the main ministries partners we have. She has never heard me preach. She has never been to one of my services. In fact, I have never even met her. Do you know why she gives to our ministry? She gives BECAUSE OF MY DADDY! She is my dad's cousin. I have never met her, but she not only supports us financially, she prays for us faithfully. What a blessing she is to our lives and ministry because of my daddy.

In 2022 my daughter, Karissa, was crowned Miss Middle Tennessee! That meant she would compete for Miss Tennessee. People began to buy ads and support her endeavor financially... because of me, her father. They'd never met her, but they knew me, and so they supported her. I love people that bless me, but if you bless my kids, I REALLY LOVE YOU!!

Fathers, most of this chapter was for you. I pray that you make it a goal to live in such a way that you make heaven, AND you take your kids with you.

If you have been wounded by a father, I pray healing over you in Jesus's name. If you are a father who has inflicted wounds on and hurt your family, repent and pursue restoration. You are playing hurt, and they are playing hurt. Take the lead. Step up. Start down the road of restoration.

Discussion questions:

1) Do you have some "father wounds?"
2) How is your relationship with your children, and how can it be improved?"
3) How can we break generational cycles of bad "father wounds?"
4) Discuss the value of "work ethic" to provide for your family.
5) Discuss the value of creating "fun times" for your family.

CHAPTER 14

NEAR THE CROSS

I LOVE SO MANY OF THE OLD HYMNS OF THE CHURCH. I HEARD THEM SO MUCH GROWING up in church that the words stuck with me. Every once in a while, the words to one of them will just pop into my head, and I will begin to sing it. The words are powerful to me, and when that happens, it always brings back precious memories of my childhood. I know we are doing mostly worship songs in our church services now, but I sure love it when we reach back and sing a hymn from time to time.

One of my favorite hymns has always been "At the Cross." One phrase especially sticks with me, the one that says, "At the cross, at the cross, where I first saw the light and the burdens of my heart rolled away . . ." Wow! How true it is!

As a follower of Jesus Christ, everything we are and hope to be is centered around these facts:

1) Jesus died on a cross for our sins
2) He was placed in a borrowed tomb
3) Three days later He came out of that tomb
4) Right now, He is seated on the right hand of God the Father, making intercession for us. Romans 8:34 says, "Who then is the one who condemns? No one. Christ Jesus who died—more than that, who was raised to life—is at the right hand of God and is also interceding for us."

PLAYING HURT... Life Hurts but God Heals

You see, the cross represents something very significant to every Christian. Jesus gave His life on the cross so that you and I might have eternal life. I am forever grateful for the cross and for Jesus.

I don't want to ever stray too far from the cross and its meaning. Even though Jesus is no longer on that cross, the significance of what took place there will always be special. I always want to be "Near the Cross"!

When I read the story of Crucifixion Day in Scripture, something really stands out to me. Let's look at John's account of Crucifixion Day...

[NIV only]

"When the soldiers crucified Jesus, they took his clothes, dividing them into four shares, one for each of them, with the undergarment remaining. This garment was seamless, woven in one piece from top to bottom. 'Let's not tear it,' they said to one another. 'Let's decide by lot who will get it.' This happened that the Scripture might be fulfilled that said, 'They divided my clothes among them and cast lots for my garment.' So, this is what the soldiers did."

Near the cross of Jesus stood his mother, his mother's sister, Mary the wife of Clopas, and Mary Magdalene. When Jesus saw his mother there, and the disciple whom he loved standing nearby, he said to her, "Woman, here is your son," and to the disciple, "Here is your mother." From that time on, this disciple took her into his home. (John 19:23–30)

I want to repeat Verse 25 here, "Near the cross of Jesus stood His mother, his mother's sister, Mary, the wife of Clopas, and Mary Magdalene." The words "NEAR THE CROSS" really get me to thinking about the people that are listed as being "near the cross." I mean, it is a short list. Why? I am sure many people were watching from a distance, but why?

Let's take a look at those that are listed as being "near the cross." I think by examining their lives we will be able to understand why they were up close that day...

FOUR ROMAN SOLDIERS

We find that there were four Roman soldiers there that day. I think it is important that we point out their presence but we need to recognize that they were there strictly out of duty. It was their job. They had done this before. To them it was the "same ole same ole." They were being paid to be there, so they performed their duties that day and that's the only reason they were there.

I have observed far too many believers who, because of the hurts and heartaches of life, have been reduced to going through the motions spiritually. Their wounds have left them numb, and they come to church out of duty. They sing songs without thinking about the meaning or even being moved by the words. They are "playing hurt." They need a healing from heaven that will break through the numbness and allow them to feel the presence of God again. Oh, I know it is not about feelings, but I do love it when I CAN feel His presence all around me. If you are reading these words right now and you have become spiritually numb to the things of God, I pray you are overwhelmed by His presence right now! He has not left you just because you cannot feel Him. Come near to Him, and He will come near to you. Amen!

MARY MAGDALENE

Mary Magdalene stood near the cross that day because it was her place of redemption. Luke 8:2 tells us that she was the woman from whom Jesus had cast out seven demons.

"... and also some women who had been cured of evil spirits and diseases: Mary (called Magdalene) from whom seven demons had come out . . ." (Luke 8:2)

Seven demons that made her do terrible things. They wrecked her life in every way. They affected her mentally, physically, and emotionally. They had one purpose in mind for her: they wanted to destroy her in every way. She was helpless and hopeless during that season of her life. She was living with constant torment and pain. It had become a way of life for her, and I am sure she was thinking that life was always going to be this way.

However, when she met Jesus, He cast the demons out and changed her life forever. The man on the cross had delivered her and redeemed her from a miserable condition. It's no wonder she stood near the cross that day. Jesus had done so much for her; she was going to be there during His darkest moments.

I was never possessed with seven demons, but I do know what it is to be bound by darkness. Even though I was raised in church, I did not serve the Lord all of my life. I know what it is to be bound by sin and have addictions control your life. However, I also know what it is to be forgiven of those sins. I know what it is to have chains of bondage fall off of me spiritually. I know what it is to be redeemed by the blood of the Lamb. Thank you, Lord, for your redemptive power! I know what that is. Mary Magdalene knew what that was. Do you know the redemptive power of God?

May we never forget what the Lord has done for us. May that keep us NEAR THE CROSS! It did Mary Magdalene. No wonder she was near the cross; it was her place of redemption.

Redemption cost a lot . . .

** For us to move from darkness to light, Jesus had to move from the light of heaven to the darkness of earth.

** For us to be delivered from guilt to forgiveness, Jesus had to be made sin for us.

** For Jesus to make us rich with blessings, He had to become the poorest of the poor.

Salome . . . place of rebuke

Most Bible commentators identify her as the wife of Zebedee and the mother of James and John. I want to remind you of a conversation she had with Jesus in Matt. 20:20–23,

20 "Then the mother of Zebedee's sons came to Jesus with her sons and, kneeling down, asked a favor of him.

21 'What is it you want?' he asked.

She said, 'Grant that one of these two sons of mine may sit at your right and the other at your left in your kingdom.'

22 'You don't know what you are asking,' Jesus said to them. 'Can you drink the cup I am going to drink?'

'We can,' they answered.

23 Jesus said to them, 'You will indeed drink from my cup, but to sit at my right or left is not for me to grant. These places belong to those for whom they have been prepared by my Father.'"

I want to focus on the selfish request she made in Verse 21, "Grant that one of these two sons of mine may sit at your right and the other at your left in your kingdom." Then Jesus made two things very clear while He was gently rebuking her:

1) You have no idea what you are asking.
2) Those places are not even mine to give.

You see, she did not understand that suffering often comes before reward. There is no crown without a cross. You must first drink the cup of suffering. Even Jesus's path to heaven came through the cross.

I believe we can all relate to her in one way or another. We, too, get selfish desires at times and have a tendency to get ahead of God. The cross can serve as a rebuke in light of our own selfish desires and requests.

One of things that I constantly feel guilty about is pursuing my selfish "wants" during my prayer time. I don't know about you, but I often catch myself "asking" God for things way more often than I "thank" Him for what I already have. I am so sorry, Lord. I don't want my prayer time to only be about "I want" or "I need." May we all remember to say, "THANK YOU LORD for the blessings in my life."

We all need conviction in our lives. I thank the Lord for it. It's during those times that I am thinking wrong, talking wrong, or acting wrong that I need the Holy Spirit to bring conviction to my heart. A conviction that leads to repentance. Sometimes the cross represents a "place of rebuke," and I am grateful for that.

MARY, MOTHER OF JESUS . . . place of reward

I cannot image the pain and heartbreak that Mary was experiencing standing near the cross. I cannot image her brokenness as she viewed her son's broken and beaten body. I cannot image the feeling she must have had knowing that she was watching her son die on a cross. She was dealing with grief and emotions she probably thought she would never have to deal with.

Let's take a look at her life and just a few events that actually brought her to this place. She was no stranger to suffering emotionally. So much suffering had brought her to this place of reward. She suffered shame and reproach when it was found out that she was with child before being married to Joseph. All of the gossip and painful words and dirty looks she got had to have been almost too much to bear. Then there was that time she had to flee Egypt to save her child, all the while knowing that many innocent children had died because of her child. Mary, the mother of Jesus, was no stranger to pain. Life hurts.

I know how bad I am when my children are sick or going through their own storms, so I cannot even imagine the way Mary felt. I know it was a hundred times worse.

So, what was her reward? Some of Jesus's last words were, "Mom, John is going to take care of you. John is going to take you in to his home and treat you like you are his mom. I have to go, Mom, but John will see that you have everything you need." (My translation of verses 26–27)

Jesus had to go, but he made sure his mom was taken care of.

Please know that the suffering you are experiencing now will come to an end, and a reward is coming to you. Stay near the cross.

JOHN . . . place of responsibility

John stood there with a different perspective. John stood there restored. You see, he along with some other disciples had forsaken Jesus and fled for their lives in the Garden of Gethsemane. However, on this day, John came near the cross, restored and forgiven. This man forgave him and restored him when he messed up; he was absolutely going to be near the cross.

Jesus gave John the responsibility of taking care of His mother. What an honor. The Scripture often talks about John being the disciple "that Jesus loved." However, when I look at that closely I discovered that it was usually John saying that, so make of that what you will.

As children of God, we also have a responsibility. We all have our gifts and callings from God. Let's give our best to the Lord; after all, He gave His best for us.

Recently I was waiting to board a plane at the Dallas/Ft. Worth airport. I was standing close to the front of the line while the passengers from the previous flight were deplaning. The last passenger to get off the plane was a man in a wheelchair who was being pushed by an airline employee. As he approached us, I could see that he was wearing a hat that identified him as a veteran. His hat actually said "WWII Vet."

As he passed us, the lady in front of me leaned over and said to the elderly gentleman, "Sir, thank you for your service." He looked up at her and with a shaky voice said, "Ma'am, I did my best." I will never forget that moment. As I minister of the Gospel AND as a Christian, I quickly thought of a spiritual analogy there. I know that one day we all will stand before the Lord. I want to be able to look at the Lord then and say, "I did my best."

So, in spite of our hurts and pains, I accept the responsibility to do what Jesus has commissioned us to do. I am "playing hurt," but I plan to stay near the cross.

*A place of redemption----it all begins at the cross

*A place of rebuke---all pride and selfishness pales in comparison to what He has done for us

*A place of reward---in our own suffering, He rewards faithfulness

*A place of responsibility---go and do the work He has called you to do

Discussion questions:

1) Discuss the power of redemption in your life
2) Have you ever been rebuked by the Lord? How did that feel?
3) Have you ever felt like the Lord rewarded you for faithfulness?
4) What is our responsibility because of what the Lord did on the cross?
5) How do you react when you see others not living "near the cross?"

Chapter 15

MISSING CHILDREN

IS JESUS A PRIORITY IN YOUR LIFE? NO, SERIOUSLY? IS JESUS NUMBER ONE IN YOUR life? I submit to you that a lot of hurts and pains that we experience are because Jesus is not number one. If HE was number one and we were listening to HIS voice, some things might be avoided.

I think we all can agree that we get way too much "junk mail" delivered to us via the postal service. I have gotten so used to it that I often toss it in the trash without even looking at it. I know that is dangerous, but I must plead guilty to it. I really should be more careful about that.

Several years ago, I went to the mailbox and pulled out a handful of junk mail. However, this time a small card that was inserted in a mail item came loose and fell to the ground. It quickly got my attention when I picked it up. There were two pictures on that card, one of a child and one of an adult. As I began to read it, I quickly discovered that these were pictures of two people that were missing. I was especially drawn to the four-year-old child that was pictured there. The more I read and looked at her picture, the more my heart broke. I pray that you or your family have never experienced anything like this.

The reality is that I cannot think of anything worse in the natural world than for one of our kids to go missing. I am a parent. I would be thinking like any parent in this situation. Are they safe? Are they warm? Are they hungry? I can also tell you that, until I found my child, all of my efforts would be put into looking for them. I would miss meals and lose sleep in an effort to find them. I would be living every day in hopes that the phone would ring, telling me my child was found safe and sound. If you are a parent, I know you feel the same way.

While in the natural world I cannot think of anything worse than a missing child, in the spiritual, I cannot think of anything worse than trying to go on without Jesus. Let me explain. I know there are a lot of places of worship that have it down to a tee. They are so gifted and talented that they can actually lead a service WITHOUT Jesus. I fear the words "having a form of godliness but denying its power." I pray you and I never reach a place where we can have a church service or live our lives without Jesus. I never want to be so "cutting edge" or "relevant" that we then expect God to keep up with us. It is still all about HIM leading and empowering us!

When I am thinking about Jesus missing from our lives, I am immediately drawn to the story in Luke 2,

"Every year Jesus's parents went to Jerusalem for the Festival of the Passover. When he was twelve years old, they went up to the festival, according to the custom. After the festival was over, while his parents were returning home, the boy Jesus stayed behind in Jerusalem, but they were unaware of it. Thinking he was in their company, they traveled on for a day. Then they began looking for him among their relatives and friends. When they did not find him, they went back to Jerusalem to look for him. After three days they found him in the temple courts, sitting among the teachers, listening to them and asking them questions. Everyone who heard him was amazed at his understanding and his answers. When his parents saw him, they were astonished. His mother said to him, 'Son, why have you treated us like this? Your father and I have been anxiously searching for you.'

'Why were you searching for me?' he asked. 'Didn't you know I had to be in my Father's house?' But they did not understand what he was saying to them.

Then he went down to Nazareth with them and was obedient to them. But his mother treasured all these things in her heart. And Jesus grew in wisdom and stature, and in favor with God and man." (Luke 2:41–52)

I have to admit, this story immediately brings up questions for me. I want to break it down before we get into the meat of the story . . .

***Scripture says that this is "annual trip," so if Jesus is twelve years old, He has made the trip twelve times.

*** On their journey home, V. 44 tells us that it was an entire day before they realized He was missing. ". . . thinking He was in their company, they traveled for a day."

***It was another day back AND another day searching for Him, so, we now have Jesus missing for three days.

***When they found Him, the Scripture says, "they were astonished." (V. 48) I just want to let you know that I cannot relate to this, is all. My mom was a wonderful and godly mom. She loved the Lord with all of her heart. However, if I went missing at twelve years old, and it was MY fault, when my mom found me, "astonished" is NOT the word I would use to describe my mom. She would be a lot of things but "astonished" isn't one of them.

The Greek word here for "astonished" is "tupto," which means "You have offended my conscience." Well, that doesn't describe my mom either, so, no, I cannot relate. Do you have a mom like mine? HAHA!

*** Then Mary asked Jesus a question, "Why have you treated us like this?" (V. 48b)

*** Jesus responded with another question, "Why were you searching for me?" (V. 49) OUCH!! I was taught to never answer my parents' questions with another question. I am feeling pain just writing this. HAHA!

***In Verse 50 we find out that Jesus's parents never did understand.

***In Verse 51a we find that Jesus was obedient to them.

Ok, we are going to move on, but before we do, I want you know how this would have read if it was about me . . .

"Lynn Wheeler was beat black and blue, grounded until he was 102 years old, and never again seen in public." HAHA!

It's just some humor folks, I am not being serious. Laughter here, that's what I am going for. LOL!

In this chapter, I want to ask five very important questions about this story:

1) WHERE DID THEY LOSE HIM?

> The Bible tells us they lost Him in Jerusalem. At that time, Jerusalem was the religious center of worship. So, they lost Him in a religious place.
>
> I understand that most people who quit serving God also quit the church. However, I have also seen a lot of people who are faithful to the church, sing in our choirs, lead a small group, and preach in our pulpits, who also have Jesus missing from their lives. It is possible to be faithful to a religious place and still lose Jesus.

2) WHEN DID THEY LOSE HIM?

They lost Him while observing religious customs. They were observing the Feast of the Passover (V. 42). Here are a couple of Old Testament reference points . . . this was a custom put into practice by Moses in Exodus 12:17 and Duet. 16:1–8. It was an annual religious custom.

This is the way we have always done it. They lost Jesus while observing these customs that they followed annually. I pray that we do not get caught up in religious customs. That we come to church or small groups and just go through the motions. May God deliver us from rut, ritual, and routine! Let's let God have control of our lives and worship gatherings. May HE cancel our agendas and take control once again.

Several years ago, I was preaching in the state of Illinois. I was standing next to the pastor during service, and he leaned over to me and said, "After this song, we will introduce you." Then he looked up to heaven and prayed this prayer, "Lord, let something happen today that is not in the bulletin." I thought he was joking, but when I looked at him, he had his eyes closed and was inwardly looking intently toward God. I agree. Let's give our worship gatherings back to God. I do not want to lose Jesus in a religious setting. You?

3) WHY DID THEY LOSE HIM?

I have to admit that this part terrifies me. It terrifies me because they didn't know they had lost Him. In V. 44 it says, "They thought that He was with them." They had become distracted and assumed He was with them.

It concerns me that so many may have lost Him but don't even know it. Distractions have caused them to lose sight of Him. It's a spiritually dangerous place to be in. If you feel like you may have lost Him, would you not take another step until you get Him back on the throne of your heart?

4) HOW DID THEY SEARCH FOR HIM?

I noticed that they immediately searched for Him among their friends and relatives. I will equate that to our "comfort zone." Ok, if we lost Him, He must be right here among the familiar. Not always. I must say that so many of the times that I have felt like that, I didn't find Him in my comfort zone. I found that I had to stretch myself outside of my comfort zone. Maybe that is what the Lord is trying to do for us all: stretch ourselves to constantly grow in Him.

5) HOW DID THEY FIND HIM?

They found Him when they returned to the place that they'd lost Him.

We have all heard the saying, "If you feel further from God than you used to, guess who moved?" God didn't move. If you feel you aren't as close to Him as you used to be or that you have quit serving Him altogether, I encourage to return to HIM! He is still your answer and your hope.

Cancel the people or things that serve as a spiritual distraction to you. They are contributing to the hurts and keeping your wounds open. Go back and find Jesus!

I say without hesitation that we cannot afford to continue our journey with Christ until we make sure He is our priority, and it is ALL ABOUT HIM! If we lose Jesus, we will become totally self-reliant.

It becomes about us. It is not about us. We need HIM more than ever. Why?

a) Because we cannot change a heart . . . I cannot do anything about a heart full of bitterness, anger, or hatred. I cannot bind up the brokenhearted or heal your wounds, BUT HE CAN!
b) We will not witness signs, wonders, and miracles . . . If our worship gatherings are about us, then the sick will not be healed and broken lives will not be restored. Only Jesus can do those things. Let's keep Him at the forefront of every service.
c) We cannot alter a person's eternal destiny . . . we cannot save the lost. Only Jesus can. Don't lose Jesus! He is vital to our daily walk and our worship gatherings.

I was preaching a Sunday-Wednesday revival crusade in Norfolk, VA, several years ago. I will never forget the Tuesday night service. Something happened to me that has never happened before. While I was preaching, a man walked into the service. He was very late, so I just thought that maybe he had to work late and was just now able to get there.

This particular church building was very long from the front to the back, so nobody saw him come in but me. He starting walking down the middle aisle, and it didn't take me long to realize . . . he was drunk. He was having to brace himself on the church pews in order to make it. I was hoping and praying that he would find a seat and be seated, but he kept coming. He walked so far down the aisle that people were now able to see him. Needless to say, I had lost everybody's attention.

He came to the second row and just stood there and stared at me. I had no choice but to acknowledge him. I asked how we could help him. I will never forget his response. He said, "Sir, I am so sorry to interrupt but I have been homeless in downtown Norfolk for many years. Tonight, I asked someone where I could go to get help. They said I could get help at this church. Can you help me?" I responded, "First of all, brother, you are not interrupting. You are the reason we are here."

Friends, if we cannot put our agenda and plans on hold to help people in need, we need to go back and find Jesus. Remember, it is ALL about Him!!

I had a couple of the church board members take the brother into the foyer and talk with him and pray with him. I continued to preach, but it wasn't long until the two board members and this man came back into the service. They were all smiling, and I could tell they had been crying. As soon as service was over, one of the board members came to me and told me that the man had prayed the sinner's prayer, and as soon as he'd said, "Amen," he'd also sobered up. So, he got saved and sober all in one prayer. Praise the Lord!!

Before I got on the plane to fly back home on Thursday, I got a report that the homeless man had got a job and a place to live! Praise the Lord!! He'd had a spiritual transformation that'd helped his other needs. He'd met Jesus and everything else had fallen into place. His pain had driven him to a place where he'd met Jesus.

I cannot do those things, and neither can you. Only Jesus can do those things. We must keep HIM as a priority, always! It is ALL about HIM!! If the Lord is number one, it helps push through the pain caused by life's circumstances.

Discussion questions:

1) Why do people struggle with the priority of keeping Jesus #1 in their life?
2) Talk about some major distractions the enemy puts in our path.
3) What are some "action steps" we can take to make sure he remains FIRST in our lives?
4) What are some "action steps" we can take to make sure He is first in our church?
5) How can we approach people that have lost their way in this area?

CHAPTER 16

THE TEST OF TRANSITION

WHEN I WAS IN SCHOOL, I HATED TEST DAY. IN FACT, I DON'T KNOW ANYONE WHO likes tests. It brings stress and anxiousness to our lives. Even if I have studied and feel like I know the material well, I am still nervous on test day. However, there is one thing that I hated worse than a test and that was a pop quiz. The "unexpected test." The test you weren't warned about or prepared for. I hated those! I know that teachers do that to make sure we are listening in class, and I usually wasn't, so I hated that surprise exam more than anything.

When I was younger, I was often called a "Youth Evangelist." I spoke at a lot of youth camps, conventions, and retreats. I enjoyed that season of my evangelistic ministry. When I wasn't doing a "youth specific" event, I would be invited to speak at Sunday services for churches somewhere in the United States. There were times when I would be visiting a city where I'd been invited to speak at a high school assembly in a public school. I had this talk that I did, I called it, "Voice your Choice," and I would speak to students about making good decisions. In the beginning, I would always try to connect with the students, so I would break the ice with a "School Prayer" I'd come across years ago. I do not even remember where I'd first heard it or read it. I'd memorized it though, and the students would always laugh when I recited it . . . the teachers, well, not so much. Anyway, it goes like this . . .

Now I lay me down to study, and I pray to the Lord that I don't go nutty. And after I've learned all this junk, I pray to the Lord that I don't flunk.

Now I lay me down to rest thinking of tomorrow's test. If I should flunk instead of pass, I pray the same for the rest of the class.

When I die, don't bury me at all; just put my bones in the study hall. Lay my books on my chest, and tell my teacher I did my best. Hahaha!

I also have come across students, especially when I was a youth pastor, who would not study for a test but would want me to pray for God to help them. I don't get it. We want God to do His part, but we don't want to do ours. I think I was supposed to pray that when they got to class, the teacher would not be there, but the answers to the tests would be lying open on her desk. I guess they wanted a Jeremiah 33:3 experience: "Thank you, Lord, that you have shown me great and mighty things that I knew not of." I somehow don't think it works that way.

Another thing we do not like is transition. Transition is that in-between season that is taking us from one place to another. We don't like leaving our "comfort zone" and moving to another place. Transitions can include job changes, church changes, geographical relocations, and moving from one house to another. I think you get the idea there. We all like our stability and comfortable places, so transition is not our favorite.

Have you ever thought about the hallway in your house or apartment? No? I hadn't either until I thought of this illustration. Please. I know it isn't exciting, but for a moment, think about the hallway in the place where you live. The hallway serves one purpose in our homes: it is transitional. The hallway transitions you from one room to another or from one place in your house to another. We don't eat there. We don't watch TV there. We don't shower there. We transition.

Maybe your time of transition seems meaningless, and you feel it serves no purpose, but be encouraged; God is taking you somewhere. Maybe you are experiencing elevated hurt and heartache during your transition, but please know that GOD IS GOD even during our seasons of transitions.

I want to take you to the life of Elijah and show you that sometimes the transition is a test.

Elijah was enjoying a good season in his life and ministry. We have all been through good seasons. We love those seasons in our lives and ministry. In fact, GOOD seasons are my favorite, and I am sure they are for you too.

Let's look at Elijah's GOOD season . . .

***He was hungry and was fed by ravens (1 Kings 17:6)

***Then he was told to find a widow at Zarephath who would take care of him (1 Kings 17:9)

***When he found her, he gave her instructions, and she followed them. Because she followed the instructions from the man of God, 1 Kings 17:15 tells us, "She went away and did as Elijah had told her. So, there was food every day for Elijah and for the woman and her family."

God is our provider! Praise God! He is meeting Elijah's need for personal nourishment. But what about his ministry? How is that going? Oh, it is a good season for that too.

***He prayed for the widow's son and God raised him from the dead. (1 Kings 17:19–22) "'Give me your son,' Elijah replied. He took him from her arms, carried him to the upper room where he was staying, and laid him on his bed. Then he cried out to the Lord, 'Lord my God, have you brought tragedy even on this widow I am staying with, by causing her son to die?'

Then he stretched himself out on the boy three times and cried out to the Lord, 'Lord, my God, let this boy's life return to him!'

The Lord heard Elijah's cry, and the boy's life returned to him and he lived."

*** Then God told him that if he would present himself to Ahab, then the drought would end . . . 1 Kings 18:1-2, "After a long time, in the third year, the word of the Lord came to Elijah: 'Go and present yourself to Ahab, and I will send rain on the land.' 2 So Elijah went to present himself to Ahab."

*** Then there was what I call "The Showdown on Mt. Carmel" with 450 prophets of Baal. God showed up BIG and silenced His enemies. 1 Kings 18:16–40, "So Obadiah went to meet Ahab and told him, and Ahab went to meet Elijah. When he saw Elijah, he said to him, 'Is that you, you troubler of Israel?'

'I have not made trouble for Israel,' Elijah replied. "But you and your father's family have. You have abandoned the Lord's commands and have followed the Baals. Now summon the people from all over Israel to meet me on Mount Carmel. And bring the four hundred and fifty prophets of Baal and the four hundred prophets of Asherah, who eat at Jezebel's table.'

So, Ahab sent word throughout all Israel and assembled the prophets on Mount Carmel. Elijah went before the people and said, 'How long will you waver between two opinions? If the Lord is God, follow him; but if Baal is God, follow him.'

But the people said nothing.

Then Elijah said to them, 'I am the only one of the Lord's prophets left, but Baal has four hundred and fifty prophets. Get two bulls for us. Let Baal's prophets choose one for themselves, and let them cut it into pieces and put it on the wood but not set fire to it. I will prepare the other bull and put it on the wood but not set fire to it. Then you call on the name of your god, and I will call on the name of the Lord. The god who answers by fire—he is God.'

Then all the people said, 'What you say is good.'

Elijah said to the prophets of Baal, 'Choose one of the bulls and prepare it first, since there are so many of you. Call on the name of your god, but do not light the fire.' So, they took the bull given them and prepared it.

Then they called on the name of Baal from morning till noon. 'Baal, answer us!' they shouted. But there was no response; no one answered. And they danced around the altar they had made.

At noon Elijah began to taunt them. 'Shout louder!' he said. 'Surely, he is a god! Perhaps he is deep in thought, or busy, or traveling. Maybe he is sleeping and must be awakened.' So, they shouted louder and slashed themselves with swords and spears, as was their custom, until their blood flowed. Midday passed, and they continued their frantic prophesying until the time for the evening sacrifice. But there was no response; no one answered, no one paid attention.

Then Elijah said to all the people, 'Come here to me.' They came to him, and he repaired the altar of the Lord, which had been torn down. Elijah took twelve stones, one for each of the tribes descended from Jacob, to whom the word of the Lord had come, saying, 'Your name shall be Israel.' With the stones he built an altar in the name of the Lord, and he dug a trench around it large enough to hold two seahs [a] of seed. He arranged the wood, cut the bull into pieces, and laid it on the wood. Then he said to them, 'Fill four large jars with water and pour it on the offering and on the wood.'

'Do it again,' he said, and they did it again.

'Do it a third time,' he ordered, and they did it the third time. The water ran down around the altar and even filled the trench.

At the time of sacrifice, the prophet Elijah stepped forward and prayed: 'Lord, the God of Abraham, Isaac, and Israel, let it be known today that you are God in Israel and that I am your servant and have done all these things at your command. Answer me, Lord, answer me, so these people will know that you, Lord, are God, and that you are turning their hearts back again.'

Then the fire of the Lord fell and burned up the sacrifice, the wood, the stones, and the soil, and also licked up the water in the trench.

When all the people saw this, they fell prostrate and cried, 'The Lord—he is God! The Lord—he is God!'

Then Elijah commanded them, 'Seize the prophets of Baal. Don't let anyone get away!' They seized them, and Elijah had them brought down to the Kishon Valley and slaughtered there."

So, we are seeing Elijah in a good season of his life and ministry. He is in both personal and corporate revival. I just love those seasons!

HERE COMES THE TEST OF TRANSITION . . .

Now we find Elijah on the run. Jezebel has found out what he did, and so Elijah is fleeing to Mt. Horeb. "Now Ahab told Jezebel everything Elijah had done and how he had killed all the prophets with the sword. So, Jezebel sent a messenger to Elijah to say, 'May the gods deal with me, be it ever so severely, if by this time tomorrow I do not make your life like that of one of them.'" (1 Kings 19:1–2)

Wow!! She must have been a mean woman. He has just defeated 450 prophets of Baal, and now a threat from one woman has him on the run. Yikes!! One woman has pulled him out of a season of provision and miracles and put him on the run. The transition has begun.

On his journey Elijah finds a tree and sits down underneath it. "... while he himself went a day's journey into the wilderness. He came to a broom bush, sat down under it, and prayed that he might die. "I have had enough, Lord," he said. "Take my life; I am no better than my ancestors." (1 Kings 19:4)

What!?!?? He's just come through a season of miracles where God was working in him and through him, but now, he is praying to die!? The transition has begun. Elijah is discouraged and depressed. He has gone from being full of faith to wanting to die. Here is the GREAT news though: GOD NEVER MISTAKES THE MAN FOR THE MOMENT! God knows that Elijah does not mean what he's said. It was a weak, discouraging moment and he said something he did not mean.

I, personally, am glad for that too. How about you? Have you ever said things to God that you did not really mean? You were discouraged, exhausted, or depressed, and things came out of your mouth that you did not really mean. It has happened to me many times. That is why I am so thankful that GOD NEVER MISTAKES THE MAN FOR THE MOMENT!

- Elijah was mentally, physically, and emotionally exhausted so he lay down under the tree and fell asleep. "Then he lay down under the bush and fell asleep.

All at once an angel touched him and said, 'Get up and eat.' He looked around, and there by his head was some bread baked over hot coals and a jar of water. He ate and drank and then lay down again.

The angel of the Lord came back a second time and touched him and said, 'Get up and eat, for the journey is too much for you.' So, he got up and ate and drank. Strengthened by that food, he traveled forty days and forty nights until he reached Horeb, the mountain of God. There he went into a cave and spent the night.

The Lord Appears to Elijah

And the word of the Lord came to him: 'What are you doing here, Elijah?' (1 Kings 19:5–9)

He was so exhausted that the angel had to wake him up just to feed him. He brought bread and water, but Elijah was so tired he fell asleep a second time. The angel had to come back and wake him up again. He gave him food and water again but this time told him, 'You are going to need strength for the journey. You need to eat.'"

Do you need strength for your journey today? Are you mentally, physically, or emotionally tired, like Elijah was? I declare over you right now that you will be strengthened for your journey. May the daily bread that God promised us be yours today. May the Word of God strengthen you today! May the rest that God promised you be yours today. Receive the strength and energy God is pouring over you right now. I pray His presence revives you and gives you a new-found strength for your journey in Jesus's name!!

Elijah received strength for the journey and he finally made it Mt. Horeb. However, when he got there, he went into the cave. God did not tell him to go into a cave. The cave represents isolation. Isolation is the devil's playground. He isolates us to defeat us. Not today, Satan!!

The Lord went in the cave after him and asked the question of him in Verse 9, "What are you doing here?" Elijah responded by complaining, which we all know gets us nowhere. WHEN YOU COMPLAIN, YOU EXPLAIN YOUR PAIN FOR NO GAIN. The Lord then gave him instructions, "The Lord said, 'Go out and stand on the mountain in the presence of the Lord, for the Lord is about to pass by.'

Then a great and powerful wind tore the mountains apart and shattered the rocks before the Lord, but the Lord was not in the wind. After the wind, there was an earthquake, but the Lord was not in the earthquake. After the earthquake came a fire, but the Lord was not in the fire. And after the fire came a gentle whisper. When Elijah heard it, he pulled his cloak over his face and went out and stood at the mouth of the cave." (1 Kings 19:11–13)

God had showed up in victory on Mt. Carmel. Then a test of transition came when he was underneath a tree, on his way to Mt. Horeb. God had used him powerfully on Mt. Carmel, but now he just wrapped himself in the cloak of the presence of God. We all enjoy the seasons of victories, but we sometimes just need to wrap ourselves in His presence again. May God help us to pass the test under the tree so we can wrap ourselves in God. We give and give, but sometimes we just need to receive so that our tank doesn't become empty. We cannot give away what we do not have.

After leaving Mt. Horeb we find that he connects with Elisha; this will be the prophet that he passes the mantle to. "So, Elijah went from there and found Elisha, son of Shaphat. He was plowing with twelve yokes of oxen, and he himself was driving the twelfth pair. Elijah went up to him and threw his cloak around him. Elisha then left his oxen and ran after Elijah. 'Let me kiss my father and mother goodbye,' he said, 'and then I will come with you.'

'Go back,' Elijah replied. 'What have I done to you?'

So, Elisha left him and went back. He took his yoke of oxen and slaughtered them. He burned the plowing equipment to cook the meat and gave it to the people, and they ate. Then he set out to follow Elijah and became his servant."

The cloak of God's presence Elijah received on Mt. Horeb had to be powerful. When Elijah placed it on Elisha, it was so powerful it made Elisha follow a man he did not even know. Symbolically we find that Elijah was passing the cloak of anointing to Elisha, who represents the next generation.

The greatest thing we can leave our kids and the next generation is the presence of God. That is more important than material things. May the next generation know the power and the presence of almighty God!

I observe some very important steps that got Elijah from Mt. Carmel to Mt. Horeb:

1) He needed personal nourishment from heaven (1 Kings 19:6)
2) He had to be willing to wait (1 Kings 19:11)
3) He had to pass the test before he went to the next level . . . the final exam . . . HE PASSED!! He passed the test even while "playing hurt."

I pray God gives you peace in your seasons of transition. Pursue His presence. Pass the test!

Discussion questions:

1) What are some "Mount Carmel" seasons in your life?
2) What are you some transitions you have struggled with?
3) How can we receive "strength for our journey," like Elijah did?
4) Why are the moments on Mt. Horeb, where he wrapped himself in God's presence, so important?
5) How can we pass that on to the next generation? Example: Elijah passed the cloak to Elisha.

CHAPTER 17

WAR OF WAITING

I CAN'T THINK OF ANY WAR REGARDING OUR INNER MAN THAT IS HARDER TO FIGHT THAN the "war of waiting." Waiting is the season between sowing and reaping. It is the season between praying and receiving your answer. Waiting is burdensome, frustrating, agitating, and just not fun.

Waiting involves patience, and this is not a strength of most people. Even if you are thinking you are a patient person, I have discovered that even people with patience prefer not to use it. LOL!

For the children of God, we must rest in the reality of God's Word, "His ways are higher than ours." It is a test of our patience because we know that quite often, God's timing and ours is different. We spend more time "waiting" on God than we do "receiving" from God. Therefore, we must win this battle in our inner man; the war between spirit and flesh that usually wants to get ahead of God. We must learn that the devil cannot control a patient man, so let's enjoy where we are while we are on our way to where we are going.

I have discovered from personal experience that the "waiting season" disrupts my peace. It is often filled with turmoil and wrestling with God. It brings a new level of exhaustion to us; however, it can also bring us closer to God. During our seasons of waiting, let's turn any negative emotion into an intentional time of getting closer to God.

*** James 5:7–11 says, "Be patient, then, brothers and sisters, until the Lord's coming. See how the farmer waits for the land to yield its valuable crop, patiently waiting for the autumn and spring rains. You too, be patient and stand firm, because the Lord's coming is near. Don't grumble against one another, brothers and sisters, or you will be judged. The Judge is standing at the door!

Brothers and sisters, as an example of patience in the face of suffering, take the prophets who spoke in the name of the Lord. 11 As you know, we count as blessed those who have persevered. You have heard of Job's perseverance and have seen what the Lord finally brought about. The Lord is full of compassion and mercy."

Lamentations 3:22-26 says, "Because of the Lord's great love we are not consumed,

for his compassions never fail.
They are new every morning;
great is your faithfulness.
I say to myself, 'The Lord is my portion;
therefore, I will wait for him.'
The Lord is good to those whose hope is in him,
to the one who seeks him;
it is good to wait quietly for the salvation of the Lord."
I want to help during your season of waiting. I have five things I want to share with you. I call these . . .

WARNINGS WHILE WE WAIT:

1) WATCH YOUR WORDS

***Proverbs 18:21 says, "The tongue has the power of life and death, and those who love it will eat its fruit."

*** Matthew 12:37 says, "For by your words you will be acquitted or condemned."

Words are powerful. Someone once said, "Words are like nitroglycerine; they can blow up bridges or heal hearts." The Word of God confirms the importance of our words because there are some three thousand references to the following . . . words, tongue, mouth, say, or speak. It is almost as if God knew how powerful words would become and how destructive they could be. When we were children, we would sing the song "Sticks and stones may break my bones, but words will never hurt me." However, that simply is not true. I can get one hundred messages and ninety-nine of them can be positive; however, it is that one negative comment or critical remark that is hard for me to get past. I try to remember that that is one person's opinion, not the majorities. Let's refuse to give that ONE PERSON that much power in our lives. They will not control our lives or thoughts. Amen?? I choose to believe what the Lord says about me.

Also, never speak words to encourage the enemy. If we speak doubt and unbelief, it will encourage the devil to continue to fight against us. Sometimes our words can give the enemy the path to our hearts, minds, and spirits. Talking like a victim seems to energize the enemy. So, let's speak faith and not doubt. Praise Him with a loud voice!

2) WATCH OUT FOR UNTHANKFULNESS

1 Thessalonians 5:18 says, "Give thanks in all circumstances; for this is God's will for you in Christ Jesus."

Ingratitude does not inspire God to hurry up the answer. It's not like He ever turns to the angels in heaven and says, "Oh no, we'd better hurry up, they are mad down there." LOL! Seriously though, we know that is not how it works. Instead, while we are waiting, we should strive to live in an atmosphere of gratitude by thanking God for what we already have and what He has already done.

I heard a story once about a little boy who was going to a friend's birthday party. So, before the party, his mom took him to the store to buy a present. As they were walking through the toy department, of course, this little boy found a toy HE wanted, not one he wanted to give as a present. His mom reminded him that they were shopping for his friend, and he could not have the toy. Well, this resulted in pouting and sulking all the way home. When they pulled up in their driveway, the little boy jumped out of the car and slammed the door. He was so mad and frustrated that he did not get what he wanted, he thought slamming the door would help. Really?

The mom in her frustration looked up to God and said, "God, I do not understand this. My children have been taught better than that. Why do they always get mad and frustrated when they don't get what they want?" God said, "I know how you feel!" OUCH!! Well, that's one of those "funny, not funny" things in life.

Remember God's delays are not always God's denials. Sometimes He isn't saying "No," He is saying, "Wait." While I wait, I choose to be grateful for how good God has already been to me!

3) WATCH YOUR ATTITUDE

I must confess that there have been times I have expressed my anger toward God because He was not moving as fast as I thought He should in certain situations. There have been times that I got ahead of God and just said, "I will do it myself." Well, that turned into a disaster! Am I the only one? Just me? Okay!

I quickly learned that DELAY IS BETTER THAN DISASTER! If I would have just waited on God instead of moving in my own way and in my own timing, I would have saved myself a lot of hurt and heartache.

There are two things here that I pray are thought-provoking to you:

a) OUR ANGER DOES NOT INTIMIDATE GOD
b) OUR SCHEDULE DOES NOT OBLIGATE GOD

Keeping our attitude in check during seasons of waiting can be challenging, but we must WIN THE WAR.

4) WATCH OUT FOR PEOPLE

That is such a general statement, so let's narrow it down. There are people that enter your life and are there for a lifetime. We all have those close to us friends that I call "forever friends." They will walk through the valleys with you without judgement.

Then we have people that God puts in our life that I call "seasonal friends." They are only in our lives for a season and sometimes for specific reason. (I will deal with this at greater length in another chapter.)

I want to ask you a very serious question. Do you have relationship discernment? Can you tell me who your true friends are as opposed to those that might be friends with you because they need something from you?

1 Corinthians 15:33 says, "Bad company corrupts good character." It does matter who you are friends with. It matters who you give permission to speak into your life. When the wrong people speak into your life, you will usually make wrong decisions.

The truth is that sometimes when the devil wants to destroy you, he will send SOMEBODY to help the process along. I am not trying to make you paranoid, but I am trying to confirm that your discerner is working in the area of relationships.

In our season of waiting, we are so desperate for a WORD from GOD that sometimes we are willing to listen to anyone and take it as words from the Lord! If the Spirit of God is speaking through SOMEONE; it will NEVER contradict the WORD OF GOD! Discern every WORD that comes your way. God uses people, but so does the devil. A TRUE WORD from GOD and HIS timing are both worth the wait.

I married late in life (thirty-five years old), and I had a lot of people trying to "fix me up" with "God's will for my life." I guess they thought I couldn't do it on my own. Anyway, if I'd listened to every person that said "God told me this person is God's will for your life," do you know how many wives I would have right now? Well, way more than the law allows.

5) WATCH OUT FOR INACTIVITY

Your seasons of waiting are not seasons of inactivity. Stay about the Father's business, and keep doing what He has called you to do. Patience works!! Some of our greatest blessings come after our longest season of waiting.

Several years ago, we spent a season of our ministry helping to raise money for church plants in the country of Ukraine. We led several teams of ministers over there as well. It was a great season of raising financing in the United States to plant churches in cities, towns, or villages that did not have a church.

One year I led a team of pastors to a small village with about two hundred people in it. It was my second trip to this village, where we planted a church. There were several grandmothers there, and they were the backbone of the church. They loved to pray, and they loved to sing. They always sang for us when we visited, and you could really feel the power of God. These ladies loved God, and they were truly grateful for a place to worship.

After the service ended, and we were all heading to the van that would take us back to our motel, we noticed these ladies were following us. Just as I was about to get into the van, my interpreter grabbed my arm and told me one of the ladies wanted to speak to me. When I turned around, she said, through my interpreter, "Thank you for coming to our village and planting a church. We (pointing at the other ladies) have been praying for this for fifty years. Fifty years?!?! Wait. What? Wow! That was a long season of waiting. That meant that since they were in their twenties, they had been praying for a church building to worship God in. So, practically all of their lives.

I, personally, cannot think of anything I have been praying for that long. That story reminds me to keep the faith and persevere in my season of waiting.

I want to show you in Scripture how seasons of waiting for us mean a busy season in the Spirit world. While we are waiting, angels are positioning themselves to minister. We cannot see it, but demons are being confronted, and a strategy is being developed.

Let me show you this example in Scripture. In Daniel 10 we find Daniel is in a waiting season. He had been praying awhile when God gives him a vision. Then something incredible happens in this chapter . . .

Daniel 10:12–13 says, "Then he continued, 'Do not be afraid, Daniel. Since the first day that you set your mind to gain understanding and to humble yourself before your God, your words were heard, and I have come in response to them. But the prince of the Persian kingdom resisted me for twenty-one days. Then Michael, one of the chief princes, came to help me, because I was detained there with the king of Persia.'"

I absolutely love this encouraging story during our waiting seasons. When the angel came to Daniel, the first thing he let Daniel know was that his prayers were heard! He told Daniel, "From the moment you started praying, we heard your prayers."

Maybe you are reading these words right now, and you are thinking the Lord is not even hearing you anymore. Maybe you feel like your prayers are not even getting past your roof. I want to encourage you with Daniel's experience. God does hear you! Keep praying! He is still your answer!

The next thing the angel told Daniel was that after he'd heard his prayer, he'd started for him with the answer. He'd been on the way, but the prince of the Persian kingdom had resisted him for twenty-one days. You see, the enemy does not want the answer to your prayer getting through. I hope this encourages you like it does me. During your waiting season, angels are fighting for you. While I am confused and sometimes frustrated, it encourages me to know that RIGHT NOW there are angels fighting on my behalf.

In Daniel's case, and perhaps in ours, it required the help of another angel (Michael) to win the victory and push it on through. However, the battle is on, and we are not fighting this alone. We may be fighting hurt, but we are fighting.

Your time is coming. The battle is being fought in the heavenly realm. Persevere. Let's do our part, and let God do His! AMEN!

Discussion questions:

1) What is the hardest thing about waiting for God?
2) Why does the "waiting season" sometimes produce anger in us?
3) Do you feel the "waiting season" is a test of your faith?
4) What does the "power of our words" have to do with waiting for God?
5) Do you verbalize your struggle in the "waiting season" or mostly keep it to yourself? Why?

CHAPTER 18

MARRIAGE BUGS

I REALIZE THERE ARE SEVERAL PEOPLE READING THIS BOOK WHO WOULD FALL INTO different categories regarding marriage:

a) Happily Married
b) Unhappily married
c) Been married but divorced
d) Been married, divorced, remarried
e) Never been married
f) Widowed
g) Widower

Regardless of which category you fall into, I think we all realize that marriage is work. I have several friends and family members who have experienced a lot of hurt and pain as a result of a broken relationship. I even know people who are in a bad marriage, which brings ongoing hurt to them. I know people that have lost a spouse they dearly loved, and the grief they experience is a constant in their lives. I am so sorry for your loss and want to express my heartfelt condolences.

We will talk about the other categories in other chapters; however, in this chapter, I want to talk to those of you who are married or thinking about marriage. I will also ask that while reading this, you do not focus on "changing your spouse" but focus instead on any changes you might need to make in your life that will affect your marriage in a positive way.

> **Marriage is not 50/50; it is two people giving 100 percent.**

Before we go any further, let's take time to read a chapter in 1 Cor. that we commonly refer to as the "love chapter" in Scripture.

(1 Cor. 13) "If I speak in the tongues of men or of angels, but do not have love, I am only a resounding gong or a clanging cymbal. If I have the gift of prophecy and can fathom all mysteries and all knowledge, and if I have a faith that can move mountains, but do not have love, I am nothing. If I give all I possess to the poor and give over my body to hardship that I may boast, but do not have love, I gain nothing.

Love is patient, love is kind. It does not envy, it does not boast, it is not proud. It does not dishonor others, it is not self-seeking, it is not easily angered, it keeps no record of wrongs. Love does not delight in evil but rejoices with the truth. It always protects, always trusts, always hopes, always perseveres.

Love never fails. But where there are prophecies, they will cease; where there are tongues, they will be stilled; where there is knowledge, it will pass away. For we know in part and we prophesy in part, but when completeness comes, what is in part disappears. When I was a child, I talked like a child, I thought like a child, I reasoned like a child. When I became a man, I put the ways of childhood behind me. For now we see only a reflection as in a mirror; then we shall see face-to-face. Now I know in part; then I shall know fully, even as I am fully known.

And now these three remain: faith, hope, and love. But the greatest of these is love."

When Paul wrote this chapter, it appears as if he forced it in between two chapters on spiritual gifts. However, the power in this chapter sounds an alarm in me about the importance of love. This chapter gives us the truest definition of love that I have ever heard.

I titled this chapter Marriage BUGS, let's look at this acronym . . .

B-----BATTLES

The enemy has been sent to steal, kill, and destroy not just our lives but also our marriages. In an effort to destroy our marriages, the enemy wants us to focus on our differences and disagreements. While we all have disagreements, let's not focus on those.

Conflict is NOT a sign you have a bad marriage. However, unresolved conflict can become dangerous. Resolve it. Now. There is a right way and a wrong way to do this. If you are going to argue, you must do it fairly.

I highly recommend that every couple reads the book "Love and Respect" by Dr. Emerson Eggerichs.[4] In his book he gives some guidelines on resolving conflict that I want to share:

- A. Avoid being hysterical . . . don't fly off the handle. Ranting and raving won't get you very far.
- B. Avoid being historical . . . don't bring up the past. Focus on that one disagreement.
- C. Fight fair . . . personal attacks and name calling are always out of line and unnecessary.
- D. Resolve the issue before moving on

***Harmful communication is all about winning the argument; helpful communication is all about solving the problem.

---

4 "Love and Respect" by Dr. Emerson Eggerichs, ©2004, used by permission of Thomas Nelson Publishing

U-UMBRELLA

I am confident we all have an umbrella, although it is rarely used. WE use it mostly when it is raining; however, I do know people that use it to shield themselves from the sun as well. The purpose of an umbrella is to protect us from the elements. It keeps us from getting wet in the rain and sunburned in the sun. In other words, it is a covering.

I believe it is the same way in a marriage: we all need to serve as a covering for our spouse at times.

"Hatred stirs up conflict, but love covers over all wrongs." (Proverbs 10:12)

"Above all, love each other deeply, because love covers over a multitude of sins." (1 Peter 4:8)

True love covers faults and fears. Let's look at a few ways we can cover our spouse:

a) Cover your spouse in embarrassing moments

When I was a young, single preacher, I remember an incident that happened one night after church. I was eating a meal at a pastor's home. There were several of us sitting around the table when the wife had to get up to get some drink refills for us. When she came back to the table and sat down, she missed her chair and fell to the floor. For some people, that would be no big deal. For her, it was!! She was a quiet and introverted individual, and this embarrassed her so bad. Her husband immediately got up and helped her back to her chair. After confirming she was alright, he began to tell a story. He began to share with the entire table about a time he had done the same thing, but in public. It was such a funny story that it immediately shifted the focus from his wife to himself. I thought that was a classy move. He covered her in her embarrassment. I loved it then, and I love it now.

Cover your spouse when they are embarrassed. Don't say or do things that will add to their embarrassment.

b) Cover your spouse in fearful moments

We all deal with our own fears and anxieties. Cover those in your spouse. My wife has things that trigger anxiety in her, and so do I. We know what the trigger is in each other, and we do not pull it; we cover it.

I am going to make a confession here. Many that are reading will think it is silly, others will think I am not very spiritual; either way, here it is. I am afraid of dogs. Yes, dogs. Now, it's not like when I see one, I scream like a girl and run, but I do sense a degree of anxiety. You see, when I was six years old, I was attacked by a German Shepherd. I still remember it even though it was more than fifty years ago. The dog tackled me and bit my leg. I still have the scar. It is an incident I cannot shake. I know you have a cute little puppy, but it looks like a German Shepherd to me. Hahaha!

I did play that up a little for humor's sake, but it is true. My wife (Dianna) knows this. She loves dogs, so every time I am put in a situation where I have to be around one, she covers me. She starts petting and talking to the dog so it doesn't bother me. I am always appreciative of that.

c) Cover your spouse in dishonoring moments

I have been around people who bash and criticize their spouse in horrible ways. This is unacceptable. Period. Don't talk about your spouse in a dishonoring way either in their presence or behind their backs. Your friends or family don't need to hear that. It will affect their feeling towards your spouse.

Instead of talking about them to other people, talk about them to God. COVER YOUR SPOUSE IN PRAYER! Pray for them every day. It will help them, and it will help you.

G---GUARDRAILS

***Guardrails are built, not grown. We have to put them in our lives so we don't fall off of the cliff. When I am driving down the road and I see a guardrail, I know that it is protecting me from something. Most of the time it is protecting me from a steep drop off or mountain. Guardrails are there for our protection, but, unlike a tree, they did not grow by themselves. Men built them, and they were strategic about their location.

I would encourage you to set boundaries inside your marriage. YOU place them there; they will not grow on their own. Boundaries must be set within yourself. In case you are not sure what I mean, I am going to give you a few boundaries that I have put in place for myself. Guardrails that I have built to protect me and my marriage. Nobody else built these, not even my wife . . .

1) My computer faces the door. My wife, or anyone for that matter, can walk in my office and immediately see what I am looking at.
2) Any email or letter that comes from the opposite sex will be read by my wife. My response will be read by my wife as well. In fact, sometimes I have her help me with the response.
3) I always show my wife "questionable" or "inappropriate" friend requests on social media. One hundred percent of the time, I do not know these people, and their pictures are not appropriate.

    DELETE!!!!!

4) Outside of my marriage, I have an accountability partner. He is also my pastor and serves on the board of Lynn Wheeler Ministries. It is an important guardrail to have. He is honest with me and asks me the hard questions at times. Accountability never works if you lie, so don't. Be honest.
5) I tell my wife where I am at all times. She doesn't demand it; I put that in place. Our spouse has a right to know where

we are at all times. If there are some concerns, communicate those. Communicate your concerns to your spouse BEFORE it becomes mistrust.
6) Financial guardrails are necessary. Never make a major purchase unless you both agree on that purchase. I would say a house, car, boat, etc. would be major purchases. I will dedicate an entire chapter to finances. I hope you read it.

Those are just some things I put into place. You do not have to do what I do; I was only helping you to "jump-start" your thoughts. Remember, YOU MUST BUILD THEM.

S----SEX

Let's go straight to the Word of God and see what the Bible says:

"But since sexual immorality is occurring, each man should have sexual relations with his own wife, and each woman with her own husband. The husband should fulfill his marital duty to his wife, and likewise the wife to her husband. The wife does not have authority over her own body but yields it to her husband. In the same way, the husband does not have authority over his own body but yields it to his wife. Do not deprive each other except perhaps by mutual consent and for a time, so that you may devote yourselves to prayer. Then come together again so that Satan will not tempt you because of your lack of self-control." (1 Cor. 7:2–5)

This is a subject that most people would rather avoid. I beg you not to ignore it. Talk openly with your spouse about it, AND do not talk to anyone else about it. Please!! Show some respect for your spouse in this area.

The Scripture is very clear on what the sexual responsibilities are for both the husband and the wife. It is incorrect to think that you can do whatever you want whenever you want in this area. Please consider your spouse in all things, including this one. If something makes them uncomfortable, don't do it.

I don't feel like I can address this subject without talking about pornography. Please know this is not optional. I have seen too many problems arise from this addiction. It is destructive to individuals and marriages. I love Paul's words to the church at Corinth:

1 Cor. 6:12 "'I have the right to do anything,'" you say—but not everything is beneficial. 'I have the right to do anything'—but I will not be mastered by anything."

Please communicate and evaluate this subject with your spouse. We don't want to be causing pain and not even know it.

My final thoughts are that SEX IS NOT A WEAPON. You do not withhold it from your spouse as a form of punishment. This has the potential to backfire in the worst way. It is wrong and contradicts Scripture, so please do not start down that road.

The goal in marriage is not to think alike but to think together. That will be especially beneficial in this area.

Please don't ever say that "marriage is just a piece of paper." So is money, but we still get up every day and work hard for it. Keep working hard on your marriage. If you are struggling in a marriage or you have been through a divorce and still feel the sting of that, I am praying you get through it soon. Broken relationships produce broken hearts, and broken hearts produce broken people, BUT GOD is the healer of the broken heart.

(Psalm 147:3) "He heals the brokenhearted and binds up their wounds."

Receive that verse today. I have.

1) Do you have addictions that affect your marriage?
2) Do you still date your spouse? Why or why not?
3) In what ways can we serve our spouse?
4) What are some guidelines for "fighting fair"?
5) If you have experienced a relational disaster or divorce, do you have an open wound that needs healing?

CHAPTER 19

MY MONEY AND MY MAKER

I REALIZE THIS CHAPTER WILL NOT BE FOR EVERYONE. I REALIZE THAT SOME OF YOU are operating your lives according to the biblical principles regarding your finances. You pay tithe. You give offerings. You are generous to the less fortunate. May God continue to bless you for your continued faithfulness and obedience. Simply put, this chapter will serve as a reminder to you of what you already know AND are putting into practice.

However, I also realize that some are drowning in debt. You got behind on your financial obligations, and it is a daily struggle to keep your head above water financially. This robs you of your peace on a daily basis. It keeps you awake at night. It never leaves your mind. This turmoil has created a sense of hopelessness for you that you feel you will never recover from. It has put you in such a bondage that you feel you will never be set free. YOU are who this chapter is for. REMEMBER THIS: nothing is ever completely hopeless as long as God is #1 in your life.

There are some things I have observed my entire ministry on the subject of finances. When you talk about money in a spiritual setting, you will get all kinds of reactions. You can feel and see some people shut down immediately. Please don't be THAT person. If we are to preach and teach the ENTIRE Word of God, then that includes finances as well.

Let's look together at some scriptural principles regarding our finances. I pray those that are struggling in this area will find some fresh revelation from God and His Word.

1) Tithing . . . returning 10 percent to God

Are you walking in obedience by returning your tithe back to the Lord? Please know that this is not about a church or a ministry getting your money; IT IS about your obedience to God. The tithe is our starting place.

Malachi 3:8–11 says, (8) "'Will a mere mortal rob God? Yet you rob me.'

'But,' you ask, 'How are we robbing you?'

'In tithes and offerings. (9) You are under a curse—your whole nation—because you are robbing me. (10) Bring the whole tithe into the storehouse, that there may be food in my house. Test me in this,' says the Lord Almighty, 'and see if I will not throw open the floodgates of heaven and pour out so much blessing that there will not be room enough to store it. (11) I will prevent pests from devouring your crops, and the vines in your fields will not drop their fruit before it is ripe,' says the Lord Almighty."

This is the only area in Scripture where the Lord tells us to "test Him." If you are not walking in obedience by tithing, I encourage you to try it. Start now. God will show Himself faithful. You might be thinking you cannot afford to, but I would say you cannot afford NOT to.

A few years ago, we got robbed. Someone broke in our house and stole some things. We reported it and after a few days, the sheriff contacted us and wanted us to come by. When he got to our house, he said that they had found the person who had stolen from us, and he was in jail. Then the sheriff said that this man has requested that we come and bail him out of jail. WHAT? He stole from us, and now he wants us to bail him out?!?! That's crazy, right??

First of all, you should know that the story is NOT true. It did not happen. I used a false illustration (don't judge, just hear me out) to illustrate a grim reality. It is ridiculous for someone that has stolen from me to expect me to bail them out. However, many people do that with the Lord. Scripture says that you are robbing God by not returning your tithe, but when you get in trouble, you still want God to bail you out. Thought-provoking. If you are not returning your tithe (10 percent of your income) to the Lord, test Him and see if it doesn't work. He wants you to.

2) Plant seed for a need . . .

Another principle taught to us in God's Word is to plant a seed (give an offering) for a specific need. This principle is taught to us in an Old Testament story found in 2 Sam. 24:18–25:

(18) "On that day Gad went to David and said to him, 'Go up and build an altar to the Lord on the threshing floor of Araunah the Jebusite.' (19) So, David went up, as the Lord had commanded through Gad. (20) When Araunah looked and saw the king and his officials coming toward him, he went out and bowed down before the king with his face to the ground.

(21) Araunah said, 'Why has my lord the king come to his servant?'

'To buy your threshing floor,' David answered, 'so I can build an altar to the Lord, that the plague on the people may be stopped.'

(22) Araunah said to David, 'Let my lord the king take whatever he wishes and offer it up. Here are oxen for the burnt offering, and here are threshing sledges and ox yokes for the wood. (23) Your Majesty, Araunah gives all this to the king.' Araunah also said to him, 'May the Lord your God accept you.'

(24) But the king replied to Araunah, "No, I insist on paying you for it. I will not sacrifice to the Lord my God burnt offerings that cost me nothing.'

So David bought the threshing floor and the oxen and paid fifty shekels[e] of silver for them. (25) David built an altar to the Lord there and sacrificed burnt offerings and fellowship offerings. Then the Lord answered his prayer in behalf of the land, and the plague on Israel was stopped."

David wanted to see the plague on the people stopped. (V. 21) He wanted to build an altar to give an offering. Araunah tried to give it to him, but he said he wouldn't take something that cost him nothing. (V. 24) He paid for the threshing floor, gave his offering, and the plague stopped. He PLANTED AN OFFERING FOR A SPECIFIC PURPOSE, and God honored his offering.

An offering is giving ABOVE your tithe. It is extra seed sown for a specific purpose. If you have a need, try it. Give an offering, and give it purpose. David exercised this principle, and the plague was stopped.

3) Power of Partnership . . .

Paul talked about partnership in Phil. 4:14–19:

(14) "Yet it was good of you to share in my troubles. (15) Moreover, as you Philippians know, in the early days of your acquaintance with the Gospel, when I set out from Macedonia, not one church shared with me in the matter of giving and receiving, except you only; (16) for even when I was in Thessalonica, you sent me aid more than once when I was in need. (17) Not that I desire your gifts; what I desire is that more be credited to your account. (18) I have received full payment and have more than enough. I am amply supplied, now that I have received from Epaphroditus the gifts you sent. They are a fragrant offering, an acceptable sacrifice, pleasing to God. (19) And my God will meet all your needs according to the riches of his glory in Christ Jesus."

When Paul mentions that the church in Philippi had sent him aid "again and again," it highlights a special partnership with them. This church has helped him more than once.

Our ministry has a group of individuals and churches who send us aid again and again. They are monthly partners who on a regular basis have joined us in helping to build the Kingdom of God. We are stronger together. These partners don't "go" but they "send." We could not do ministry at a level that we do it without them. Their generosity fuels us to reach more people for God.

When I first got out of college and became an evangelist (traveling minister), I had a conversation with a seasoned evangelist who had been traveling many years. We talked about a lot of things that day, including finances. I will never forget what he said to me regarding that subject: "Lynn, we aren't in the ministry for money, but without money you won't be in the ministry long." It takes money to reach people for God. I believe if everyone would pay tithe and partner with a ministry, the church would never have to say "no" to any ministry need.

Oh yes, before I transition to the next subject, I do practice what I preach. We support four missionaries and two evangelists on a monthly basis. Consistent giving brings a consistent harvest. There is POWER IN PARTNERSHIP!!

4) EXPECTATION . . .

Luke 6:38 says, "Give, and it will be given to you. A good measure, pressed down, shaken together, and running over, will be poured into your lap. For with the measure you use, it will be measured to you."

I heard someone say one time that we "don't give to get but we give to give." I love that.

The principles of God cannot be stopped. If you give, it will be given back to you. Then we give again. The process continues to repeat itself. So always give with the expectation that God will do what He said He would do.

5) The Issac Offering . . .

While I am only going to reference a few verses, I would encourage you to read the entire story of Abraham and Isaac in Genesis 22. It is a story of trusting God on a level that most of us cannot reach.

God had told Abraham to take his son, Isaac, to a mountain and sacrifice him there (V. 2) After a few days they arrived at the mountain, and Abraham strapped him on an altar with full intentions of sacrificing his son. However, as he reached for the knife, the angel stopped him, and God provided a ram that was caught in the thicket instead. (V. 12–13)

(12) "Do not lay a hand on the boy," he said. "Do not do anything to him. Now I know that you fear God, because you have not withheld from me your son, your only son."

(13) Abraham looked up and there in a thicket he saw a ram[a] caught by its horns. He went over and took the ram and sacrificed it as a burnt offering instead of his son.

The principle of the "Isaac offering" is when you give to God, and HE IMMEDIATELY gives it back to you. We all love when God responds quickly, right? Granted, this isn't always the case, but it was in this case. That's why I call it an "Isaac offering."

Several years ago, I was preaching in Memphis, TN. We had a great meeting, and after service, the pastor asked me to come into his office. We both sat down, and he proceeded to tell me that the Lord had told him to give me a ring that he had on. He told me how much it was worth and said he wanted me to have it. Although I was very moved by his generosity, I immediately heard the Spirit of God say to me, "ISAAC OFFERING; give it back to him." I took the ring and told him what God had said to me. I handed him the ring back, and he broke into tears. He proceeded to tell me why it was such a valued possession, and believe me, the value was much more than the cost of the ring. I told him God was testing his obedience, and he'd passed the test. It was a powerful moment for both of us.

Sometimes the Lord brings finances or possessions our way so we can pass them on. You see, God won't give it to us unless He can get it through us. I know this isn't always the case, but sometimes God might want to get something through us. This is just another part of God's giving system in Scripture.

I find that people generally fall into one of four categories when talking about finances and Scripture:

1) They were never taught about giving.
2) They were taught WRONG about giving.
3) They ignored what they were taught about giving.
4) They responded to what they were taught about giving.

If finances are a source of turmoil for you, and you find yourself in debt and struggling to make ends meet, look to God's Word. Activate HIS principles in your life. I realize there are some great financial books with some great ideas in them, but there is nothing like the Word of God in this area.

I want to encourage you today. Apply biblical principles and believe God for a turnaround. If you do your part, He will do His. He will supply all of your needs according to His riches in glory. May God turn your pain toward His promises today and give you back what has been lost or stolen. If you are in a bad spot because of your own bad decisions, remember, God's grace is sufficient for you.

I want to close this chapter by just listing some verses that you can lean on in this area:

(6) Remember this: Whoever sows sparingly will also reap sparingly, and whoever sows generously will also reap generously. (7) Each of you should give what you have decided in your heart to give, not reluctantly or under compulsion, for God loves a cheerful giver. (8) And God is able to bless you abundantly, so that in all things at all times, having all that you need, you will abound in every good work. (9) As it is written:

"They have freely scattered their gifts to the poor;
their righteousness endures forever."

(10) Now he who supplies seed to the sower and bread for food will also supply and increase your store of seed and will enlarge the harvest of your righteousness. (11) You will be enriched in every way so that you can be generous on every occasion, and through us your generosity will result in thanksgiving to God." (2 Cor. 9:6–11)

"But remember the Lord your God, for it is he who gives you the ability to produce wealth, and so confirms his covenant, which he swore to your ancestors, as it is today." (Deut. 8:18)

"A gift opens the way for a giver and ushers him into the presence of the great." (Proverbs 18:16)

"For the Lord your God will bless you as he has promised, and you will lend to many nations but will borrow from none. You will rule over many nations, but none will rule over you." (Deut. 15:6)

Discussion questions:

1) Why is paying tithe so important?
2) Why is sowing financial seed so important?
3) What does it mean to be "generous"? More than money?
4) Has God ever performed a financial miracle for you?
5) Is the bondage of debt a spiritual battle?

CHAPTER 20

RELATIONAL REALIGNMENTS

I THINK WE ALL UNDERSTAND AND HAVE EXPERIENCED THE FACT THAT THERE IS A difference in friends and TRUE friends. Some people come into our life for a SEASON, but everyone comes into our life for a REASON. Some people were not assigned to you forever. There were no hard feelings. Nobody did anything wrong, but their season in your life ended. Maybe they helped you through a tough time similar to one they had been through. Maybe they mentored you as far as they could. Maybe you had a common interest or you relocated. There are a lot of reasons, and not all of them bad, why some relationships end.

On the other hand, there are relationships that ended for a glaring reason. It was hard and hurtful. It wounded you, and you are still feeling the pain of the cut. Here are a few things that come to the forefront under these circumstances:

***Unkind words were spoken
***Wounding actions occurred
***Good things were undone
***There was complete misunderstanding

I think we all have this in common regarding this subject . . . we have all been hurt, and we have all inflicted pain on others. Maybe you need to pause and ask yourself, "Who have I hurt?" and "Have I made a biblical effort to restore that relationship?" Maybe you can make a phone call or schedule a lunch appointment to make things right. If it in your power to bring reconciliation, do it.

However, sometimes this is not in our power. Sometimes we have no idea what happened. Did I say or do something that drove this person away from me? I have discovered that people don't need our permission to exit our lives. They just do. Most of the time it isn't anything we said or did . . . they just left. In other words, their season was up. Maybe you didn't see it that way, but they did. Let them go. You could possibly harm your relationship by holding on.

We will all be received the way we are perceived. Maybe your perception was that this was a lifetime relationship, but they didn't see it that way. In marriage, it takes TWO people who WANT to be married to each other to make it work. In all other relationships, it is the same. BOTH people have to WANT to remain close. If even one person doesn't, then it isn't going to happen.

I know many people have been hurt by broken relationships. You are not responsible for what others have done to you; you are responsible for what you have done to others.

To this day I am still struggling with something that happened over ten years ago in my life and ministry. I got an email from a pastor's secretary asking me to remove him from my mailing list as they did not want to receive any communication from my ministry at all. I had preached for this pastor in another church he had pastored and considered him a friend. I had no idea what I had done. I know there might be pastors reading this that say, "We get so much mail from ministries, and it just piles up." I get that; however, I was a friend . . . or at least I thought so.

I did the biblical thing and reached out to him. I asked if we could meet for coffee or lunch and that I was buying. Crickets. I tried again about three months later. Crickets. I know he read my messages because they were sent on social media. I could see that he'd read them.

There are times when you simply do not understand why someone has exited your life. In fact, you may never know. It's okay. It hurts, but we move on. We play hurt sometimes. This is one of those times.

PLEASE KNOW THIS . . . just because you admit to being hurt or confused by "relational realignments" does not mean you have bitterness or unforgiveness in your heart. You were hurt. I was hurt. We move forward and do not allow it to affect our other relationships. You can be hurt. It's okay. Bitterness is not okay. Unforgiveness is not okay.

> "Many people will walk in and out of your life, but only true friends will leave a footprint on your heart." (Eleanor Roosevelt)

***Let's take a look at relationships together:

1) JESUS CHRIST

. . . this is the #1 relationship in our life. Spend time growing in this relationship daily. If you keep this relationship strong, it will help you with all of your other relationships. Relationships strengthen as you spend time together. Spend time with Jesus. Often. Guard that time well. Spend time with Him personally and corporately.

2) SPOUSE

I recently heard a story about a son talking to his dad. He said, "Dad, I recently heard that in ancient China a man doesn't even know his wife until they marry." The dad quickly replied, "Son, that's not just true in China, that is true EVERYWHERE."

We have all heard that you don't really know your someone until you live with them. I think the "other" truth is that you don't really know yourself either.

Only second to our relationship with the Lord, is our relationship with our spouse. The Word of God tells us to love, honor and respect them. I would also add that we should walk in forgiveness as well.

Matthew 19:6 says, "So they are no longer two, but one flesh. Therefore, what God has joined together, let no one separate."

3) FAMILY

I didn't want to put just children in this category; I wanted to put "family." I do believe that the children are the priority under this category though.

We have been entrusted with our children by God. The Bible tells us they are a gift. They don't ALWAYS feel like a "gift," but they are. Pray over them and speak blessings over them every day. The Bible encourages us to train them as well.

Proverbs 22:6:

"Start children off on the way they should go, and even when they are old, they will not turn from it."

Ephesians 6:4:

"Fathers, do not exasperate your children; instead, bring them up in the training and instruction of the Lord."

We are to prepare our children for life, not protect them from it. Life is full of hurts and heartache, but if we have taught them that the Lord can make a way for them during the dark times, we have succeeded. If they leave our nest prepared spiritually, everything else will take care of itself. Make that your priority. Do it while you are their number one influencer. Someday you won't be. You will always be their parent, but not always their number one.

After our children, I believe that other family members are next. God did not just save Noah; He saved his family too.

I hear so many stories and pray for so many people regarding their family relationships. I hear stories about relatives who refuse to show up for the holidays because they cannot get along with other family members. It is a shame and very heart-breaking.

I understand that many people feel justified in their actions or lack thereof. The question we must ask ourselves is NOT "Will I be around them?" The question that matters is, "Have I forgiven them?" We must forgive because the Bible says we must. Not because a preacher says it or because you are reading it in this book, but because the Bible says it.

The next step after forgiveness is restoration. Once true forgiveness happens, the relationship can be restored. I didn't say you have to be best friends or even super close, but I know firsthand the power of restoration in family relationships. I went through seasons of broken relationship with some close family members. I know the power of forgiveness and the power of restoration. We do not have any idea what tomorrow will bring. Don't stay mad or hold grudges too long. Don't worry about the friends or family members that don't like you. Enjoy the ones that love you.

Your story is different from mine. Your pain level or sense of betrayal may be different than mine. Only you know what has happened; however, when you reach out, keep in mind that they may perceive things totally different. If you desire restoration or need to forgive a family member, try these steps:

a) **Communicate**
b) **Resolve**
c) **Restore**

It may not go smoothly, but go for it anyway. It is important now and for future generations in your family. If you are not received, then you have done all you can do. Put it in God's hands and keep moving forward. God can heal you and your heart without restoring the relationship. If you have done all you can do, then it is now on them. My family has heard me say many times, "All you can do is all you can do."

The next group I want to talk about is FRIENDS; no, wait, TRUE FRIENDS. True friends are honest with you one-hundred percent of the time. They don't mind telling you when you are wrong. Even if you have a disagreement with them, they love you anyway. True friends are few and far between. Find your circle that won't leave you when you fail or struggle at times. You NEED them.

They are there for accountability, so don't get angry when they call you out on something. They may advise you differently than you thought they would, but a TRUE friend will tell you the truth. They are a confidant, and they won't tell anyone everything they know about you. They can be trusted. Find those two or three people in your life.

Proverbs 17:17 says, "A friend loves at all times,
and a brother is born for a time of adversity."

Proverbs 27:17 says, "As iron sharpens iron,
so, one person sharpens another."

Find those people who will love you not matter what and will sharpen you when you are around them. When you do, those are your TRUE friends.

Then there are other people in your life that are acquaintances. You may see them occasionally for a meal or enjoying an activity together. You enjoy hanging out with them and might even call them a friend, but they are not your "go to" person when you are experiencing hard times. We all have those people in our lives, and we also NEED those people in our lives.

Enjoy. Have fun. These are casual friends that you may have connected with through common interests, activities, or beliefs. I have many friends that fall into this category. I love them and value our time together. However, these people seem to move in and out of my life from time to time. It's not because anyone gets mad or hurt; it's just life.

"I am of the age where many of my friends are starting to retire. There are many pastors that I have preached for through the years, who are now retired. I no longer see them as often as I once did. I miss these people. I miss hanging out with them. However, from time to time our paths may cross, and it is ALL GOOD. We laugh, joke and often pick right up where we left off during our last visit. Please don't worry about those relationships that change just because "life happens." It is just a different season of life. Nothing more. Nothing less. Do you have relational experiences like that too?

The final relationship I want to talk about is mentorship. I believe it is very important to have a mentor AND to be a mentor. Unfortunately, I did not have a mentor in my early days of ministry. As I reflect on that now, I realize I needed one desperately. It would have saved me a lot of hurt, heartache, and mistakes when I was a young minister. If you are young, seek out a mentor. You do not know it all, and you do need advice and guidance from those who have walked the road before you. If a mentor does not cross your path, then seek one out. Find a wise and trusted counselor in your field and listen to them. It will save you from making a lot of unnecessary mistakes.

You will not find the word "mentor" in the Bible. However, I have heard many ministers share the following examples of it:

**Moses was mentored by his father-in-law Jethro (Exodus 18)
**Eli advised Samuel (1 Samuel 1–4)
**Jesus mentored His disciples (Luke 9)
**Paul mentored Timothy (1 and 2 Timothy)

I did finally discover the joys and benefits of having a mentor, and it has been a tremendous blessing to me. I have discovered that every sheep needs a shepherd.

Be a Barnabas . . . always looking for someone to encourage
Look for a Paul . . . someone to watch and learn from
Train a Timothy . . . do not keep what you know to yourself; invest it others

I have also discovered that there will come a day when a "reverse mentorship" takes over. I have mentored young people that have grown beyond me. After all, that is the goal. They are now in a place where they can mentor me. I have people that help me "stay young." They help me navigate social media and take advantage of all of the ministry opportunities that are available to me beyond just preaching in churches. The people I once mentored are now mentoring me. They are a huge blessing in my life and ministry now. I love the way the Lord uses those relationships to come full circle.

Relationships are vital to life and our walk with the Lord. If you are struggling in any of the areas we have talked about, pursue a solution to resolving the conflict. Broken relationships inflict pain. The wounds need healing. Only God can bring that. Maybe you feel like you are "playing hurt" in the area of relationships. I pray that the Lord will heal your wounds. I pray you feel the presence of the Lord even as you are reading this right now. He is a healer!!!

Discussion questions:

1) Is there unresolved conflict in your relationships? What are some action steps you can take to resolve it?
2) Is there a friend or family member you need to forgive? Apologize to?
3) How does our relationship with the Lord affect all other relationships?
4) What is the value of having or being a mentor?
5) How can I improve in the area of relationships?

REFERENCES

***All scripture is from the New International Version, published by Zondervan